Sewing Techniques for Theatre

Sewing Techniques for Theatre: An Essential Guide for Beginners distills the intimidating art of sewing down into simple, quick, and effective lessons to prepare readers for an entry-level position in a costume shop. The lessons follow an hour-by-hour structure, offering detailed instructions to creating 11 sewing samples, a scrub shirt, and a tote bag. Embedded in the projects' directions are lecture materials on safety, irons, fabric, and patterns. With a wealth of hands-on exercises, review questions, photographs, and step-by-step instructions for compiling a portfolio, this guide teaches aspiring costume technicians about the culture and machinery of the costume shop, and equips them with the necessary skills to begin their career as members of a costume shop team.

Tracey Lyons is an Instructor and Costume Designer at the University of Wisconsin–Whitewater. Her professional scope includes design in classical and contemporary theatre, dance, opera, and musicals. She coauthored *Teaching Introduction to Theatrical Design: A Process Based Syllabus in Costumes, Scenery, and Lighting* (Routledge 2016). She holds an M.F.A. in Costume Design and Technology from Wayne State University and a B.A. from the College of Saint Benedict / Saint John's University.

Sewing Techniques for Theatre

An Essential Guide for Beginners

Tracey Lyons

NEW YORK AND LONDON

First published 2019
by Routledge
52 Vanderbilt Avenue, New York, NY 10017

and by Routledge
2 Park Square, Milton Park, Abingdon, Oxon, OX14 4RN

Routledge is an imprint of the Taylor & Francis Group, an informa business

© 2019 Taylor & Francis

The right of Tracey Lyons to be identified as author of this work has been asserted by her in accordance with sections 77 and 78 of the Copyright, Designs and Patents Act 1988.

All rights reserved. No part of this book may be reprinted or reproduced or utilized in any form or by any electronic, mechanical, or other means, now known or hereafter invented, including photocopying and recording, or in any information storage or retrieval system, without permission in writing from the publishers.

Trademark notice: Product or corporate names may be trademarks or registered trademarks, and are used only for identification and explanation without intent to infringe.

Library of Congress Cataloging-in-Publication Data
Names: Lyons, Tracey, author.
Title: Sewing techniques for theatre : an essential guide for beginners / Tracey Lyons.
Description: New York, NY : Routledge, 2019. | Includes index.
Identifiers: LCCN 2018058388 (print) | LCCN 2018060216 (ebook) | ISBN 9780429946493 (Adobe Reader) | ISBN 9780429946479 (Mobipocket Unencrypted) | ISBN 9780429946486 (ePub3) | ISBN 9781138596450 (hardback : alk. paper) | ISBN 9781138596467 (pbk. : alk. paper) | ISBN 9780429487620 (ebook)
Subjects: LCSH: Sewing—Technique. | Costume.
Classification: LCC TT705 (ebook) | LCC TT705 .L96 2019 (print) | DDC 646.4/78—dc23
LC record available at https://lccn.loc.gov/2018058388

ISBN: 978-1-138-59645-0 (hbk)
ISBN: 978-1-138-59646-7 (pbk)
ISBN: 978-0-429-48762-0 (ebk)

Typeset in Gill Sans
by Apex CoVantage, LLC

CONTENTS

Acknowledgments   ix
Introduction   xi

CHAPTER 1   HOUR ONE   1
Introduction to the Costume Shop   1
Shop Safety   3
Review   4
HOUR TWO   4
Fabric   5
   Fabric Shopping   8
   Divide the Fabric   8
Introduction to the Overlock Sewing Machine   11
   Practice Using the Overlock Machine   13
Introduction to the Portfolio   16
Review   17

CHAPTER 2   HOUR THREE   19
Overlock Machine   20
Sewing Notions   21
   Thread   21
   Needles   21
      Threading the Needle   21
   Buttons   24
      Shank Button   24

	Sewing Sample #1. Part 1 of 2 – Shank Button	24
	Flat Button	28
	Sewing Sample #1. Part 2 of 2 – Flat Button	28
	HOUR FOUR	32
	Irons	32
	Hook and Bar	32
	Sewing Sample #2. Part 1 of 4 – Bar	32
	Sewing Sample #2. Part 2 of 4 – Hook	36
	Snap	38
	Sewing Sample #2. Part 3 of 4 – Socket	39
	Sewing Sample #2. Part 4 of 4 – Stud	41
	HOUR FIVE	44
	Right and Wrong Side of Fabric	44
	Hemming Stitches	46
	Whip Stitch	46
	Sewing Sample #3. Whip Stitch	47
	Slip Stitch	50
	Sewing Sample #4. Slip Stitch	50
	Review	53
CHAPTER 3	HOUR SIX	55
	Introduction to Sewing Machines	56
	Threading the Sewing Machine	58
	Machine Stitching Projects	59
	Sewing the Straight Stitch Seam	59
	Sewing Sample #5. Straight Stitch	60
	Straight Stitch Seam With Top Stitching	67
	Sewing Sample #6. Straight Stitch With Top Stitching	68
	HOUR SEVEN	71
	Curved Seams	71
	Concave Curve	73
	Sewing Sample #7. Concave Curve	73
	Convex Curve	77

	Sewing Sample #8. Convex Curve	77
	90° Corner	80
	Sewing Sample #9. 90° Corner	81
	HOUR EIGHT	85
	Dart	85
	Sewing Sample #10. Dart	86
	Hemming With Bias Tape	94
	Sewing Sample #11. Hemming With Bias Tape	95
	Review	97
CHAPTER 4	HOUR NINE	99
	Introducing the Scrub Shirt	99
	Reading a Pattern	100
	Laying Out and Cutting the Shirt	102
	HOUR TEN	109
	Constructing the Shirt	109
	Overlock	109
	Stitch Shoulder Seams	110
	Stitching Shoulder Seams on Facings	112
	HOUR ELEVEN	113
	Finishing the Neck Edge	113
	HOUR TWELVE	121
	Pinning and Attaching the Sleeves	121
	Stitching Side Seams	124
	HOUR THIRTEEN	128
	Hemming the Sleeves	128
	Shirttail Hemming the Bottom	129
	Hemming the Side Vents	130
	Review	133
CHAPTER 5	HOUR FOURTEEN	135
	Tote Bag	136
	HOUR FIFTEEN	144

Portfolio	144
Portfolio Requirements	144
Conclusion	146
Review	146
MASTER SUPPLY LIST	147
CHAPTER REVIEW ANSWERS	149
Index	153

ACKNOWLEDGMENTS

Deconstructing the costume construction business has been a group endeavor. To Damon Jay Photography, Bernina International AG, and Simplicity Patterns, thank you for your trust and contributions. These amazing students at the University of Wisconsin–Whitewater made this book possible: Kelsey Mattos, Hope O'Reilly, Ashley Brouwer, Alexa Farrell, Emily Ottinger, Dustin Peterson, Abrya Schneeberg, Carlee Wuchterl, Heather Wallman, Abigail Smith, Jordan Meyer, and Kory Friend. Special thanks to Annie Kailhofer who helped with this book and *Teaching Introduction to Theatrical Design*. From teachers of mine, to editors and family (Bill, Elizabeth, Spencer), my gratitude is enormous.

INTRODUCTION

Now more than ever, live theatre, movies, mini-series, and television feature breathtaking visuals. Aspiring costume creators strive to join a team of industry innovators. Even my first-year college students want to build period garments for upcoming plays. Many books aim to strengthen stitching skills, build corsets, and pattern doublets. These offerings leave a gap between the desire to create and entry-level skills. What about the catch-22 of, "You need skills to get a job, and you need a job to get some skills?" How can students turn their college costume shop practicum hours into a skill set strong enough to build a portfolio that contains the proof of basic stitching and garment construction necessary to land their first costume shop job? How can an ambitious non-college artisan learn sewing?

Here you can jump-start your experience. This text is an introduction to basic stitching skills. By starting all students at a beginning level and quickly developing a common language of words and actions, the projects build a solid foundation. Think of these exercises as a piano player would think of doing scales. It is great to have the skills then use them to develop your own style. This is the launching point for your own creativity.

Analogous to the projects within the book are narratives on important aspects of costuming. Although reading about a subject will lead to knowledge, to know sewing is to embody it through doing. Work the sewing samples, scrub shirt, and tote bag in the order presented. Back up to review as necessary.

THE STRUCTURE OF THE BOOK

Germinating from a 5-week course that meets for three 1-hour periods, the book is divided into 15 separate hours. For the reader, the hours create benchmarks for progress and time estimations. It should also serve as a reminder that sewing skills quickly develop.

Just like my class, this book gives a detailed explanation for each project. An outline format presents the assignments in logical progressions. Within the subcategories are helpful advice and clarifications. The numbering within the framework starts over with each new sewing sample, finishing process, and scrub shirt section. Read the whole section first and then begin the stitching from the first step.

In Chapters 1 through 3, 11 sewing samples are created. Chapter 4 tackles the scrub shirt. (If the Simplicity pattern goes out of print, several five-piece shirt designs could substitute.) Chapter 5 covers both the tote bag and portfolio. Each project contains some new and some review material. The explanations on the revisited steps streamline to emphasize the new. Step back and return to earlier sections as necessary.

Italicized words or phrases acknowledge new terminology. Information within the same section contains an explanation of the item.

Occasionally, I have included a "Pro Tip" section. These non-sequiturs cover a variety of topics and are meant to give a bit of insight about the costume construction industry.

Mark up this book. Write in the margins. Cross off steps as you complete them. Underline and highlight topics worth your review. Note your own tips and tricks. Think of this as a recipe book with the option to personalize.

CHAPTER 1
HOUR ONE

INTRODUCTION TO THE COSTUME SHOP

Welcome to the costume shop. This Narnia – a magical place within the 'closet' – is a hub of creation and creative people. Most costume shops combine the fields of clothing construction, millinery (hat construction), wigs/facial hair, masks, fabric dyeing/manipulation, makeup, and all things that could fit into the category of costume crafts. Usually, every person within the shop is working on a unique piece.

Because of this variety, a costume shop can be a strange place for a novice. Not only is it full to the brim, it is thick with rules, ritual, and culture. It is normal to be overwhelmed. Be patient with yourself and with others when beginning this adventure. Know that the projects covered in this book will provide a common set of skills and vocabulary that allow you to jump into your new environment.

People are the most important part of a costume shop. When entering say, "Hello." Introduce yourself. Forming questions in an entirely new environment is difficult, and you should feel free to ask or just listen, depending on your comfort level.

Your first day is just that, one of many – simply a start of a great journey. A re-occurring theme in this book and in costume shop work is, "You won't learn everything all at once." Become familiar with the shop from the big picture down to the details. Does each area have a primary use? What is the flow of a costume's construction? Learn the various storage areas too. Tour the facilities. Often, working in the costume shop can feel like cooking in someone else's kitchen; you may have skills, but finding the tools is difficult. Is there an experienced shop worker to pair with and form a team? Assist by gathering supplies for the project and later putting them away, thus learning the location of the scissors, thread, needles, and other items while benefiting from observing the work of the senior partner. Soon enough, you will be working solo on projects, and this mentor will be available to help with questions.

Creativity thrives among those with good work ethics. Come to work on time and prepared to participate. Give plenty of notice when canceling or re-scheduling. Call when you are not able to come to work. Know when the shop is facing a deadline and how your actions will affect the process of creating the show. Treat coworkers with kindness. Ideally, a shop should be devoid of harmful gossip. There are still plenty of people to talk about, such as tacky celebrities or your crazy aunt. Yes, sometimes an eye roll escapes, and it takes more effort to count blessings than to complain. Knowing that you can hold your tongue about others can build trust among colleagues. Other HR guidelines will also apply.

FIGURE 1.1 *A spray booth is more of a necessity than a luxury. Work in a properly ventilated area*

FIGURE 1.2 *Dye vat with ventilation hood*

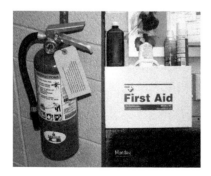

FIGURE 1.3 *Where does your shop keep first-aid and fire suppression items?*

SHOP SAFETY

Maintaining a safe shop is everyone's responsibility. If you adhere to the following precautions, you will be well on your way to working in and creating an optimal atmosphere. Dress appropriately. Wear non-slip, full-coverage shoes. Stains, paints, and dyes ruin clothes, so dress to mess. Hair, scarves, ties, jewelry, and other hanging items catch in projects and cause problems.

Sprays, paints, glues, or anything emitting a smell needs proper ventilation. A spray booth draws odors and toxins out of the shop (see Figure 1.1). Even items that do not smell may have a particulate hazard, such as granulated fabric dye. Note the vent hood over the dye vat on Figure 1.2. Observe the manufacturer's warnings on products.

Identify the safety equipment. Locate the fire extinguisher and first aid kit in preparation for fire or injury. Figure 1.3 depicts these items in an area with easy accessibility.

Perhaps your costume shop has a written set of rules. If they aren't posted, ask the shop supervisor for clarification. In all cases, let your good sense prevail. The most effective precaution might be your state of mind. Be alert.

Even the occasional party has boundaries, yet they remain 100% necessary. In my shop, celebrations underscore the accomplishments of the staff, create a community, and allow time to reflect on the breadth and depth of the work. To prevent staining the costumes, place them a safe distance from food. Properly store all toxic chemicals during cooking or serving. What are the rules in your shop for food and beverages when having a party? What are the rules for food when not having a party?

REVIEW

True/False

_____ Millinery and crafts are never done in a costume shop.

_____ Sewing machines are the most important things in a shop.

_____ Partnering with an experienced stitcher can be helpful in the short and long term.

_____ Safety is the responsibility of the costume shop manager.

_____ Costume shops should celebrate their accomplishments.

HOUR TWO

Costume construction is a hands-on skill; to learn it, you must do it. The book alternates between lecture and projects, growing your skills logically. Read each section and note the corresponding photographs. Complete each exercise before moving on. To facilitate smooth transitions from project to project, start each chapter with all of the recommended supplies. A cumulative list is located at the end of the book.

NECESSARY SUPPLIES FOR CHAPTER 1

Fabric scissors

Thread scissors

Measuring tape

Chalk

1 yard of woven fabric – see details in the "Fabric Shopping" section

Overlock sewing machine

SCAVENGER HUNT

Try finding the location of the following items in your costume shop:
- Thread scissors (about 4" long)
- Thread
- Hand sewing needles
- Fire extinguisher
- First-aid kit

FABRIC

When constructing garments, our medium for the art is the fabric. In broad strokes, we can divide fabric into four categories; leather, felt, knit, and woven (see Figure 1.5). Leather is animal hide after processing. Leather can be difficult (but not impossible) for

FIGURE 1.5 *From left to right: leather, felt, knit, and woven fabric*

use in costume construction. Felt begins as fibers (often from wool) soaked, smashed, and heated into an even layer. It is easily shaped and provides insulation so long as it isn't re-soaked, re-smashed, or re-heated. Knit fabric starts with fibers spun into a yarn, looped in succession to develop a garment or yardage. Knits have stretch and can form well to the body. Woven fabric also begins with yarn, layered with alternating strands perpendicularly. Weaving often happens on a loom.

Woven fabric is the most accessible entry into costume construction. The 11 exercises, the scrub shirt, and the tote bag from this book are created using woven fabric. Many of the same techniques taught here will work on other types of fabric; simply allow your skills to advance before taking on the more difficult materials.

There are some descriptive terms pertinent to the use of woven fabric: selvage, grain, cross grain, and bias (see Figure 1.6). The subsequent subdividing of the fabric will also use these terms.

FIGURE 1.6 *Terms used to describe directions associated with the weave of the fabric*

Grain / Grainline (Warp) – all threads parallel to the selvage. The threads in the loom. This direction has the least amount of stretch.

Cross Grain (Woof) – all threads perpendicular to the selvage. The threads that integrate into the threads in the loom. Some fabric has a little stretch in the cross grain.

Bias – the 45° angle from the grain. Can be either a forward slant or backward slant. This direction fosters the greatest amount of stretch in fabric.

Selvage – the tightly woven manufacturers' edge of the fabric.

Fabric Shopping

Use woven fabric for the 11 upcoming projects. Fabric sold in major stores usually comes 45" or 60" wide (the measurement from selvage to selvage). Purchase the length of fabric by the yard (36") or fraction of a yard. The projects in this chapter and the next require at least 30" × 40" of fabric. At the cutting table, buy five-sixths of a yard or 30" of either 45" or 60" wide fabric. A word of caution: since the store will cut the fabric with scissors, the edge of that fabric will not be perfectly on the cross grain (see Figure 1.7). Later, when you tear the fabric on the cross grain to straighten the edge, you will reduce your yardage. Since exactly 30" is needed, buy a little extra at the cutting table to allow for this "shrinkage."

When I teach this course, I am able to provide fabric for students. Using the leftover fabric pieces from previously constructed garments upcycles and declutters the shop.

> **PRO TIP**
>
> I was shopping at a Vogue Fabrics in Chicago, Illinois, and after purchasing a dozen different cuts of fabric, the shop worker asked, "Are you a costume designer?" "Yes. How did you know?" I replied, and she answered, "Costume designers always round up to the next full yard when purchasing fabric."

FIGURE 1.7 *The cut edge of the fabric is not exactly on the cross grain*

Divide the Fabric

These steps divide your fabric, first into three strips and then each strip into five rectangles. Ultimately, these 15 rectangles create the 11 stitching samples outlined in this book. Set aside your larger scraps.

Create three strips of 10" wide fabric (see Figures 1.8–1.13).

1. Use scissors to cut in about 1" and tear on the cross grain to square up the edge of the fabric
2. Measure along the selvage 10"
3. Make a small mark with chalk
4. At the mark, cut through the selvage
5. Tear on the cross grain
6. Again, measure a second 10" strip and make a mark with chalk
7. At the mark, cut through the selvage and tear on the cross grain
8. For the third time, measure 10" along the selvage, mark with chalk, and tear the third strip on the cross grain

FIGURE 1.8 *Cut through the selvage and tear along the crossgrain to even the edge*

FIGURE 1.9 *With chalk, mark at 10" intervals*

FIGURE 1.10 *Clip and tear at 10" intervals to create three strips*

FIGURE 1.11 *Step 9 removes the selvage*

FIGURE 1.12 *Measure and mark at 8" intervals*

FIGURE 1.13 *Clip and tear at 8" intervals*

On each of the three strips, apply the following steps:

9. Remove the selvage by cutting in from the edge 1". Use that opening to tear along the grain
10. Measure along the cross grain. Mark the strip at 8" intervals using chalk
    a. This creates five rectangles per strip of fabric
    b. There will be scrap fabric
11. Cut using scissors to start the tear and divide each strip

(Repeat steps 9–11 on the other two strips)

12. Your final result is 15 rectangles, each measuring 8" × 10"
    a. Expect a slight decrease in the measurement if the fabric frays. Having exact measurements is not important
13. Save the scraps for future practice on the overlock machine

PRO TIP

Cut off the selvage, because the weave is tighter and can launder or iron differently than the body of the fabric, thus causing puckering or pulling. Sometimes, the selvage is not printed or treated in the same way as the body of the fabric. Only in desperate situations would I include selvage in a project or garment.

FIGURE 1.14 *The printing leaves the selvage exposed*

INTRODUCTION TO THE OVERLOCK SEWING MACHINE

Each piece of equipment in the costume shop serves the stitcher in different ways. This type of machine has many names (overlock, overlocker, serger, merrow) as well as many functions and advantages (see Figure 1.15). Often a favorite of the novice stitcher, the overlock is easy and fun to use. Since longevity, future

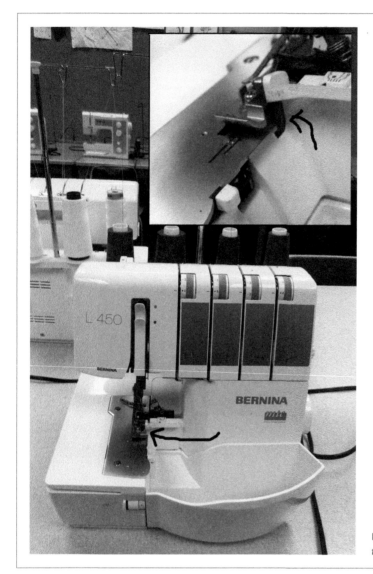

FIGURE 1.15 *The arrows point to the upper and lower knives*

size alterations, and extreme wear are of high consideration for the shop, an overlock becomes necessary in costume construction.

Everyone has contemporary garments, especially knits, constructed with an overlock machine. Look at the seams on a T-shirt for an example of this finish.

First, it is fast and efficient because it sews and seals the edges of the fabric simultaneously. Second, because the overlock uses three or more cones of thread, sewn fabric will stretch without breaking the stitches. Third, some garments have finished edges without traditional hems, simply finished with an exposed overlock stitch. Many overlock machines have settings for rolled hems or 'lace' finishes – consult the manual when you are ready for these advanced settings.

When learning this machine, identify the upper knife – i.e., chopping blade. Because there is no auto shutoff, it could cut your finger as easily as it cuts fabric. Pay attention to your hand placement. Avoid distractions while operating. Other key parts of the overlock machine are shown in Figure 1.16.

It is the norm in my shop to overlock all pieces of a garment immediately after cutting. By preventing fraying on each piece of fabric, the costume alters easily and lasts longer.

Practice Using the Overlock Machine

Using the scrap pieces from the division of the fabric, practice and experiment, working to build your comfort with the overlock machine (see Figures 1.17 and 1.18).

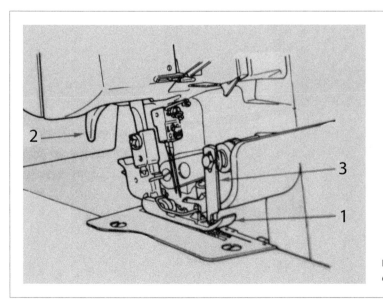

1. Presser foot
2. Presser foot lifter
3. Upper knife

FIGURE 1.16 *Parts of the overlock machine:*

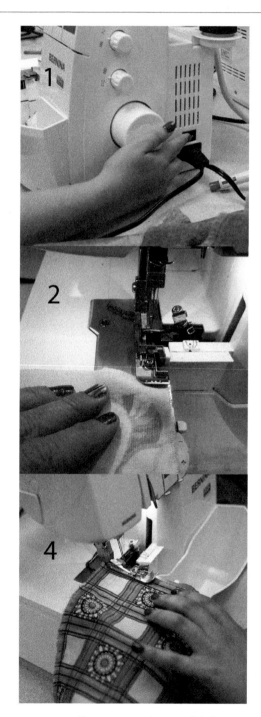

FIGURE 1.17 *Photos correspond to steps 1, 2, 4*

1. Power on the machine
2. Starting with a scrap of woven fabric, set the edge of the fabric against the front of the presser foot (near the needle) of the machine
3. Gently press your foot down on the foot pedal (gas pedal) to draw the fabric through the machine
4. The fabric should catch and be propelled at a rate correlating with the pressure from your foot
   a. Keep your fingers safe by monitoring their proximity to the upper knife

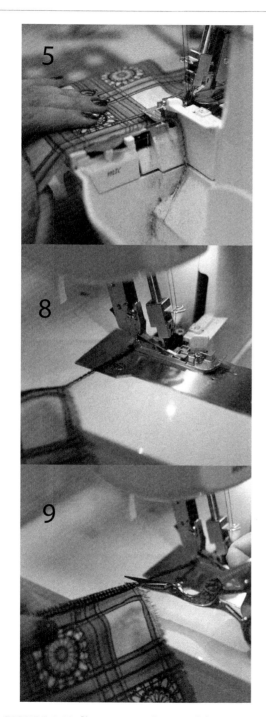

FIGURE 1.18 *Photos correspond to steps 5, 8, 9*

5. How far to the right can you place your fabric without cutting into it?
6. If you intend to trim just the fray from the fabric, where should you site the fabric?
7. When you have completed overlocking a side of your scrap fabric, don't raise the presser foot
8. Continue with your foot pedal until a little trail of thread forms behind the fabric
9. Trim close to the fabric and leave a long thread chain hanging from the machine
10. Trim the thread chain close to the fabric at the starting edge of the overlock stitches

> **PRO TIP**
>
> There are alternatives to overlocking.
> 1. Pinking shears or pinking scissors cut small 45° angles. The bias cuts reduce fraying
> 2. Regular (non-overlock or straight stitch) sewing machines have a variable width setting. To prevent fraying, sew near the cut edge with a wide stitch. This is a zigzag stitch. It does work similarly to the overlock by wrapping threads around the cut edge
>
>
>
> **FIGURE 1.19** *Left to right: small inside corner, edges finished with pinking shears, edges finished with zigzag stitch*

INTRODUCTION TO THE PORTFOLIO

Theatrical artists communicate their skills using a portfolio (see Figure 1.20). Formatted in different ways (spiral binder, PowerPoint, or website), it is a collection of projects and images portraying the journey and accomplishments of the artist. Even though the portfolio is a tool for a job candidate to use during an interview, the most frequent audience is you; make the portfolio to satisfy your taste. Since your work will not be complete until the end of the book, the portfolio assignment is last. Of course, you could look ahead to Chapter 5 for detailed information and start setting up your portfolio earlier.

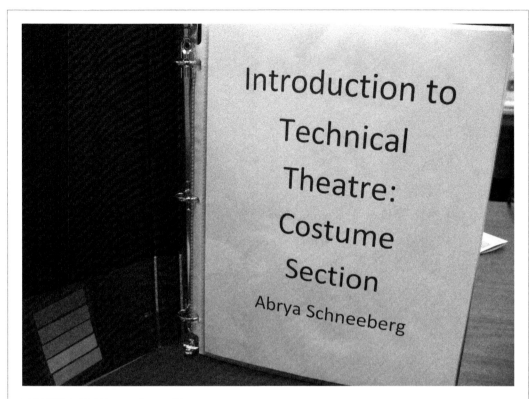

FIGURE 1.20 *Title page for portfolio*

REVIEW

True/False

_____ This book divides fabric into four basic types.

_____ The grain of the fabric has more stretch than the bias.

_____ The bias has less stretch than the cross grain.

_____ The overlock machine has an auto shutoff to prevent cuts.

_____ The overlock machine only has one cone of thread.

CHAPTER 2

HOUR THREE

Chapters 2 and 3 contain instructions for the 11 sewing samples worked on the 15 rectangles of woven fabric. In application to the samples, Chapter 2 reviews the overlock machine and expands the topic of fabric. There are sections on irons and sewing notions too. Each sewing sample is broken down into several steps with accompanying pictures. Save your work for placement in your portfolio (introduced in Chapter 1 and detailed in Chapter 5).

NECESSARY SUPPLIES FOR CHAPTER 2*

Thread

Hand sewing needle

Flat button – four holes

Shank button

Snap (two parts)

Skirt hook and bar

Seam gauge

Pins

Iron

*Plus previously introduced supplies

OVERLOCK MACHINE

It is time to return to the mechanics of the overlock machine. Prepare the 15 rectangles for use by overlocking all edges on each piece (see Figure 2.2).

1. Power on the overlock machine
2. Locate the foot pedal
3. Lower the presser foot
4. Align the fabric at the front of the presser foot and near the upper knife
5. Check the placement of your hands to ensure their safety from the knife
6. Push down the foot pedal. Speed is regulated by the pressure from your foot
7. As the fabric advances, note the amount trimmed by the upper knife
    a. Optimally, only the fray is trimmed off of the fabric
8. Sew past the end of the fabric to leave a thread chain
9. Trim the thread near the garment and leave the chain on the machine
10. Trim the thread from the beginning of the overlock stitching

Overlock each edge from start to finish. Remove and shift the fabric to begin overlocking the next edge. Rounding the edges diminishes the accuracy of the cutting. Finish the edges on all 15 rectangles.

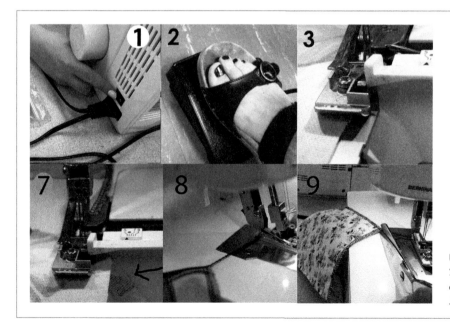

FIGURE 2.2 *The pictures detail steps 1, 2, 3, 7, 8, and 9*

SEWING NOTIONS

The term *notions* means 'stuff for sewing.' There is an inference that notions are small, but that is not a defining characteristic. The long list of things that are notions would include, but not be limited to, thread, needles, buttons, snaps, measuring tapes, chalk, pins, and ribbon. Fabric, machines, scissors, irons, and patterns are not considered notions and yet very much 'stuff for sewing.' Sewing Sample #1 and Sample #2 attach notions to the rectangles in a way that simulates their use on a costume.

Thread

Any sewing topic could ignite several chapters of information and discussion. Such is the case with thread. I'm going to skip past most of the debate and simply recommend that new stitchers use a basic spool (not cone) of all-propose thread available from fabric retailers. As your skill set increases, so will your experience with thread. In no time, you may be demanding pre-waxed and pre-cut boutique-brand sewing thread. For the purposes of the following assignments, lengths of thread are about 36″.

Needles

This book will discuss both *sewing machine needles* and *hand sewing needles*. Hand sewing needles have a point at one end and the eye (hole) at the opposite. Machine needles have the point and eye at the same end, and the other end inserts into the machine. In either case, thin needles create less resistance when drawn through fabric yet risk breaking if too strained. Specific to hand sewing, start these projects with a size 7, 8, or 9 needle. Try different sizes to learn your own preferences.

THREADING THE NEEDLE

In preparation for the upcoming hand sewing projects, these steps demonstrate the process of threading a needle and tying a knot. The first introduction of a new skill is very detailed. Later, the abbreviated description defers to a new set of skills. Feel free to return to previous sections for review.

Tracey Lyons

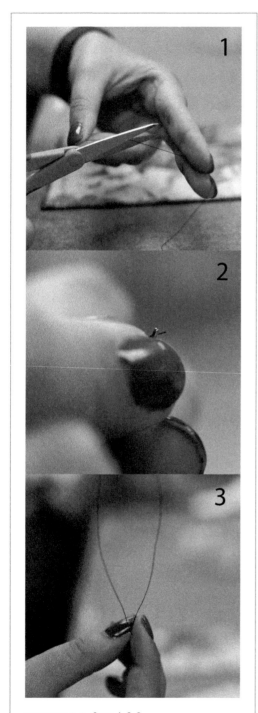

FIGURE 2.3 Steps 1, 2, 3

Threading the needle (see Figure 2.3):
1. Cut 36" of thread
2. Insert one end into the eye of the needle
   a. A fresh cut on the thread or a cut at an angle can improve the chances of hitting your mark
3. Bring the ends of the thread together

Tie the knot at the ends of the thread using these steps (see Figure 2.4):

4. Loop the thread, crossing the ends with the middle of the thread
5. Wrap the ends through the loop a couple of times
   a. More wraps mean bigger knots that hold well, even in a loosely woven fabric, but can be lumpy. Find the right balance for your project
6. Pull the ends of the thread to close up the loop
   a. It takes a little practice to place the knot near the ends of the thread
7. If the thread following the knot is long or uneven, trim to about ⅓"

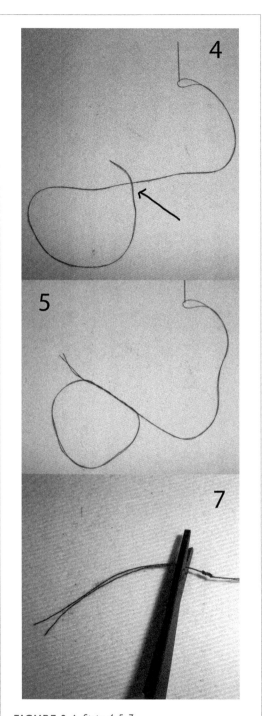

FIGURE 2.4 *Steps 4, 5, 7*

> **PRO TIP**
>
> It may help to consider the dominate hand as the controller for the needle and thread. The recessive hand controls the fabric.

Buttons

Buttons have decorated garments for thousands of years. Because of their history, they are a critical part of costume construction.

Shank Button

The first of the two types of buttons discussed in this book is the shank.

Opposite the button's face, on the underside, is a loop or lump called a *shank*. The shank lifts the button away from the garment allowing room for the buttonhole layer to fit comfortably under the button.

Sewing Sample #1. Part 1 of 2 – Shank Button

Follow this process to attach the shank button to the rectangle of fabric (see Figures 2.5–2.7):

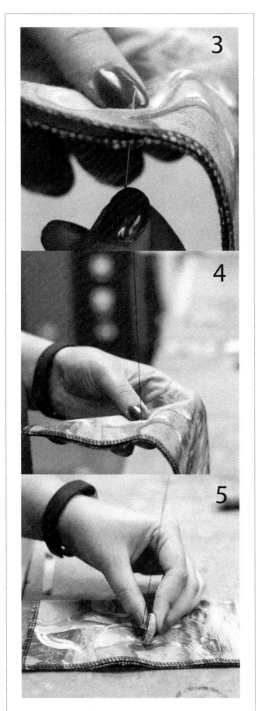

FIGURE 2.5 *Steps 3, 4, 5*

1. Fold an 8″ × 10″ rectangle of fabric in half on the length
   a. This creates a double layer of fabric for the button applications
   b. Both the flat and shank buttons will be sewn onto this square
2. Draw two dots (in our shop, we often use chalk for marking fabric, but for this assignment, anything will work) several inches apart on the same side of the rectangle to use as guides for sewing the flat and the shank buttons
3. With a threaded needle, start from the back of the fabric and penetrate the fabric behind the chalk mark with the needle only
   a. Back out the needle if it didn't strike close to the mark indicating the button placement
4. When confident of the accuracy, draw the needle and thread through the fabric until stopped by the knot at the end of the thread
5. Bring the needle through the shank of the button

FIGURE 2.6 *Steps 8, 12, 13*

6. Stitch back through the fabric near but not exactly on the previous stitch
7. Pull until snug but not tight
   a. Tight stitches can pucker and pull fabric out of shape
8. Repeat the process of stitching from the back of the fabric, through the shank, and return through the fabric to the back at least three times
   a. Mind the button to avoid spinning
9. Finish with the needle drawn to the back of the fabric opposite the button

    The shank button and all the hand stitching in this book finishes with a knot and then a stitch to 'bury the knot.' Follow the next steps for the process:

10. Knot the thread by bringing the needle through to the back of the fabric (still on the opposite side of the fabric from the button)
11. Start a stitch that grabs a few threads and keeps the needle to the back of the fabric
12. Pull the needle free of the fabric but do not tighten the thread, leaving a loop
13. Bring the needle through that thread loop a couple of times
    a. This wrapping of the needle with thread creates the knot

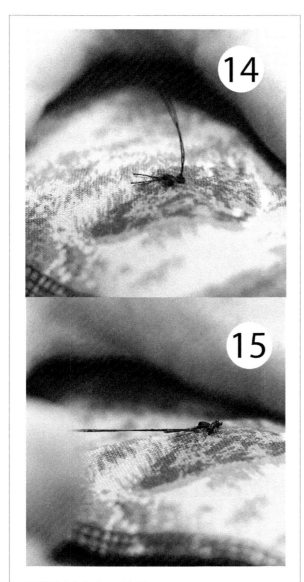

FIGURE 2.7 *Steps 14, 15*

14. Pull the needle, bringing the wrapped section against the fabric
15. As an added measure of security, 'bury the knot'
    a. To bury the knot, take one last stitch through a tiny bit of fabric near the knot, keeping to the back of the fabric
    b. This stitch secures the top of your previous knot and locks it to the garment
16. Trim your thread close to the fabric, but not too close (about $3/16$th of an inch)

> **MARKING FABRIC WITH CHALK OR WAX?**
>
> In my college program, the costume shop had black wax available to mark garments. I loved its vivid and easy flow. Even after repeated scolding, I would use nothing else. Sure, it didn't come off of the garment easily (or ever) but my love was deep. Some things are a preference: chalk or wax, other things in a costume shop conform strictly to industry standards. Learn your preferences by trying new things. Develop your skills so that you can conscientiously break the rules.

Flat Button

A flat button has two or four holes. They lay much closer to the garment. The following stitching technique lifts the button to accommodate the buttonhole layer.

Sewing Sample #1. Part 2 of 2 – Flat Button

Attach the flat button to the second button placement mark located on the folded fabric rectangle previously used for the shank button (see Figures 2.8 and 2.9).

Chapter 2 Hour Three   29

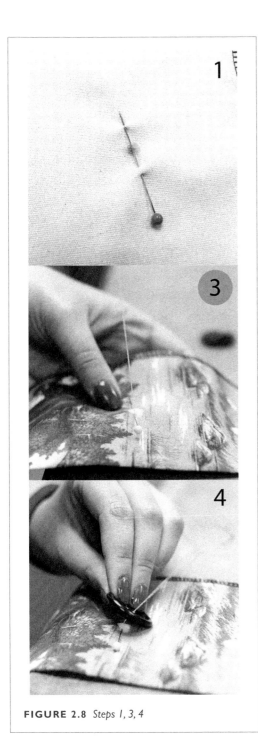

FIGURE 2.8 *Steps 1, 3, 4*

1. Begin the process with a straight pin embedded into the fabric directly above the button placement mark
   a. From the top of the fabric (on the side where you will sew the button) pin in and out of the fabric preceding the mark. Travel over the mark and pin in and out of the fabric on the opposite side of the mark
2. Using a threaded needle, start from the back of the fabric
3. Draw the needle and thread up next to the straight pin until stopped by the knot
4. Bring the needle through one of the drilled holes on the button
5. Place the button over the pin with the holes (either one pair or two) straddling the straight pin

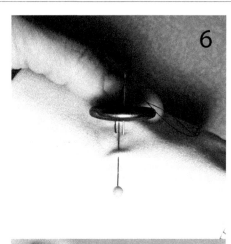

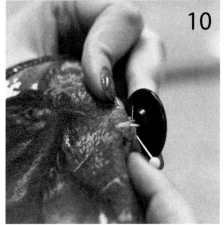

FIGURE 2.9 *Steps 6, 8, 10*

6. Draw the needle back down through the hole and fabric on the opposite side of the pin
   a. Making two parallel rows of stitches is stronger and less bulky than a stitch pattern that makes an X
7. Sew from back to front, front to back through this pair of drilled holes three times
8. Switch to the remaining pair of drilled holes
9. Sew from back to front, front to back, three times through these holes too
10. Make a stitch that brings the needle and thread between the button and the fabric. Create a thread shank by following these steps (see Figure 2.10).

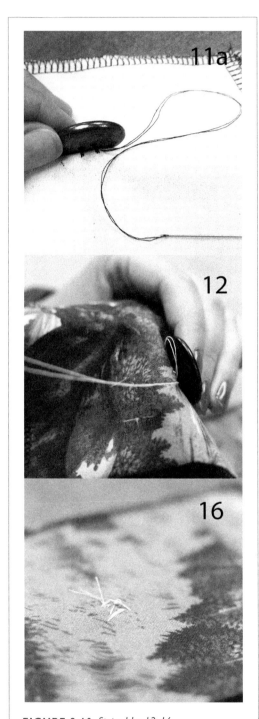

FIGURE 2.10 Steps 11a, 12, 16

11. Remove the straight pin
    a. Notice the long stitches between the fabric and the button
12. With the thread on your needle, wrap around the long stitches in the gap between the button and fabric
    a. Circle the long threads three times
13. Draw the needle through to the back of the fabric, opposite the button
14. Knot the thread
15. Bury the knot
16. Trim the threads

Set aside this and all of the sewing samples for placement into your portfolio.

FIGURE 2.11 *Sewing Sample #1 finished*

HOUR FOUR

IRONS

Burns are the most frequent injury in my costume shop, and they are preventable. As with all things, safety should be your priority. Never operate this or any machinery that has damage. Know the correct and safe heat settings. Mind the steam, which is hotter than the iron. Use the iron within the manufacturers' recommendations. Power off the irons when the shop is not in use.

At this point in the book, the projects will require frequent ironing. Ironing or 'pressing' improves the quality and finished look of a garment. It is labor intensive and very transformative. Try ironing the remaining 14 rectangles. The flattened fabric is easier to manage.

Hook and Bar

Hook-and-bar fasteners create an invisible closure on costumes. This book describes the steps to sew a *skirt hook and bar*. The sewing skills for the skirt style are applicable to other hook-and-bar closures that you will encounter while working in a costume shop.

Sewing Sample #2. Part 1 of 4 – Bar

The hook and bar will be attached to the same pair of rectangles as the snap (directions for the snap will follow).

FIGURE 2.12 *Steps 3, 5, 7*

Follow this process to attach the bar (see Figures 2.12–2.14):

1. Iron two rectangles lengthwise
   a. The folded edges will overlap when the hook and bar combine
2. Designate one rectangle "lower layer" and the other "upper layer"
3. On the lower layer, set the bar back from the fold of the fabric – about an inch is normal on a garment
4. Place the bar with the drilled holes smooth to the fabric and the center of the bar arching away from the fabric
   a. With your recessive hand, hold the bar to the fabric. The dominate manages the threaded needle
5. Begin from the back and stitch through the fabric and through one of the drilled holes at the end of the bar
6. Pull until stopped by the knot
7. Stitch back down through the fabric, outside of the bar, near the drilled hole, not the adjacent drilled hole

FIGURE 2.13 *Steps 9, 12, 13*

8. Snug up the stitch
9. Repeat the in and out a minimum of three times
10. Switch to the adjacent drilled hole, stitching up through the fabric and the hole
11. Stitch down through the fabric near this hole
12. Repeat the in and out a minimum of three times
13. Travel from this pair of holes to the ones on the other end of the bar.
    a. Stitch into ONE layer of fabric and bring the needle out of the fabric near the unsewn end of the bar
    b. This is a big, yet discreet, stitch
    c. Sew the bar this way to prevent thread hooking and tearing, thus undoing your stitches and leaving the garment without a means to close

Chapter 2 Hour Four   **35**

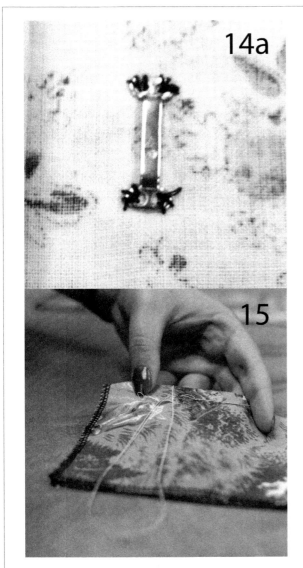

FIGURE 2.14 *Steps 14, 15*

14. Stitch the other pair of drilled holes (similar to steps 5–12)
    a. Each pair of drilled holes should have at least three sets of stitches
15. Make your knot on the backside, opposite the bar
16. Bury the knot; trim threads

FIGURE 2.15 Steps 1, 2, 3

Sewing Sample #2. Part 2 of 4 – Hook

The following steps guide in the attachment of the skirt hook (see Figures 2.15 and 2.16):

1. On the underside of the rectangle designated 'upper layer,' place the back of the hook parallel and close to the folded edge of fabric
   a. Imagine a pair of slacks where the bar has been sewn to one side of the fly, the hook is on the underside of the opposite side
   b. The flat side of the hook is against the fabric
2. The first stitch starts on the same side of the hook and next to the center hole
   a. The needle penetrates both layers of fabric and returns inside of the large center hole of the hook
   b. The stitches used to attach a hook are visible from the outside of the garment and need to look tidy
3. Repeat in and out of the fabric at the center hole three times
   a. Make consecutive stitches small and close together

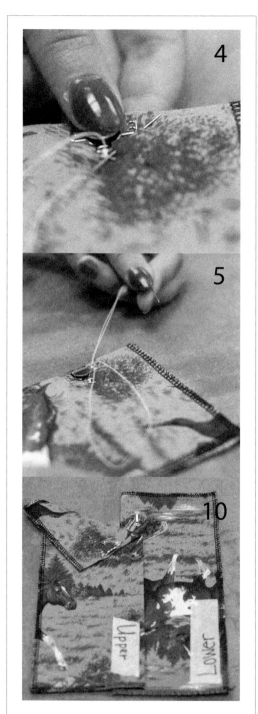

FIGURE 2.16 *Steps 4, 5, 10*

4. To travel from the center of the hook to a pair of drilled holes at the top, stitch between the layers of fabric (or stitch on the same side as the hook but NOT on the opposite side because a long stitch on that side will show on the finished garment)
5. Stitch the drilled holes at the top of the hook in the same manner as the pair of holes in the bar
6. Make a big discreet stitch to switch to the opposite pair of drilled holes on the hook
7. Stitch each of the two remaining drilled holes three times each
8. Make your knot on the same side as the hook
9. Bury the knot
10. Trim the thread close, but not too close

Snap

Snaps come in all sizes and in a couple of different shapes. A snap has two parts: the 'stud' and the 'socket' (see Figure 2.17). In a practical application, the costume's weight and the strain on the snap should determine the size needed (bigger snaps create a stronger hold). Test the snap parts prior to stitching to ensure that you have a match before stitching. Unsnap and attach each half separately using the following directions.

FIGURE 2.17 *Left to right: stud, socket*

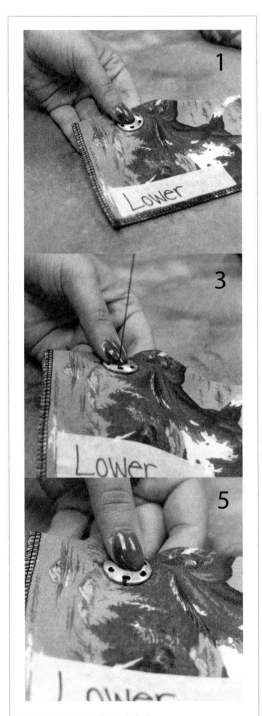

FIGURE 2.18 *Steps 1, 3, 5*

Sewing Sample #2. Part 3 of 4 – Socket

Use the same pair of fabric rectangles as the skirt hook and bar (see Figures 2.18–2.19).

1. On the lower layer (the one with the bar attached), begin with the socket against fabric
   a. Note that when placed upside down, the socket half of the snap can look very similar to the stud half of the snap
   b. The snap will not click shut unless corresponding faces touch
2. Hold the snap half to the fabric with your recessive hand
3. With a threaded needle, stitch from the back of the fabric
   a. Pull the needle through the fabric and into a drilled hole from back to front
4. Stitch down through the fabric outside of the snap from front to back
5. Repeat at least three times

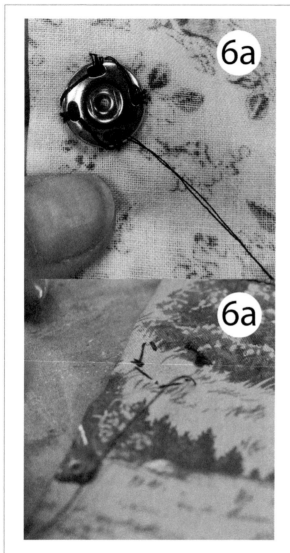

FIGURE 2.19 *Step 6a with travel threads on the snap side, and step 6a with travel threads on the underside of the snap*

6. Move to the next drilled hole
   a. Threads that 'travel' from one hole to the next can be made on either side of the fabric
7. Each drilled hole is sewn a minimum of three times
8. Knot the thread on the backside
9. Bury knot
10. Trim threads

Sewing Sample #2. Part 4 of 4 — Stud

Before sewing the stud half to the top layer, test and check for correct placement. Once again, the fabric side of this attachment will show to the audience. Stitches on the right side (opposite the stud) should be small and tidy.

FIGURE 2.20 *Steps 1, 3, 5*

The following steps detail attaching the stud to the fabric (see Figures 2.20 and 2.21):

1. Begin with the fabric and snap held by the recessive hand
2. Near a drilled hole, stitch from the snap side through both layers of fabric
3. Neatly return the needle to the snap side, landing inside of a drilled hole
4. Repeat this step at least three times per drilled hole
5. Place stitches that 'travel' from one hole to the next on the snap side or hide the stitch between the two layers of fabric

6. Knot on the snap side
7. Bury knot
8. Trim threads

FIGURE 2.21 *Steps 6, 8*

Set aside this and all of the sewing samples for placement into your portfolio.

FIGURE 2.22
Sewing Sample #2 finished

HOUR FIVE

RIGHT AND WRONG SIDE OF FABRIC

So far, this book has discussed measuring, dividing, overlocking, and manufacturing fabric. Now take a closer look at a single piece of fabric. Most fabrics (but not all) have one side designed to be the finished or outer side. For example, quilting fabric is often a cotton with a printed side intended to be the exterior (see Figure 2.23). This 'designed' side is the *right side* and the other the *wrong side*. For the purposes of the following exercises, we will use the right side of the fabric for the outside of the sewing samples.

FIGURE 2.23 *The right side of the fabric has a vivid print*

PRO TIP

The difference between the right and wrong sides of fabric can be subtle. When cutting this type of fabric for the purposes of making a costume, I will place pieces of masking tape on the right side of each piece. The tape helps to keep the right sides identified and removes quickly from the finished garment.

Fabrics without any difference between right or wrong sides can be tricky. First, the right and wrong sides may appear identical in one light but in another, such as stage lighting, the right and wrong sides may look noticeably different. Another pitfall of this fabric lies with the construction. Without the ability to identify the right sides, you could be building some parts with wrong sides together and some with right sides together. There is even the chance that you could build two left sides of a garment instead of the intended right and left.

There are exceptions to using the right side of the fabric on the

> outside of the garment. Once, while creating a costume that needed to look old, I used the wrong side of the fabric for the outside, as it was duller in color and looked worn out.

HEMMING STITCHES

Hems are the finished edges on the garment's sleeve, pant leg, skirt, and other places. This bit of fabric turned to the inside requires specific stitches to hold it in place. Sewing Sample #3 (Figure 2.27) and Sample #4 (Figure 2.31) detail two types of frequently used hemming stitches. As with most of this book, understanding these basics build a foundation needed for more advanced projects.

Whip Stitch

Fast and secure, the whip stitch is a costume shop 'go-to' for hemming and repairs. Although beautiful and tidy on the outside of a garment, the inside shows a great deal of thread from the stitches. Whip stitches shouldn't be used if the garment will be seen inside out or taken off while on stage.

Sewing Sample #3. Whip Stitch

The following steps detail the whip stitch (see Figures 2.24–2.26):

1. On one rectangle, fold up 2" of the 10" length toward the wrong side of the fabric
   a. The amount past the fold of the hem is the *hem allowance*
   b. A *seam gauge* is a small metal ruler used to measure the depth of the fold
2. Make another narrow fold that tucks the overlocked edge into the hem allowance
   a. Pin through all layers if desired
3. The first stitch with a threaded needle places the knot on the folded edge of the hem allowance

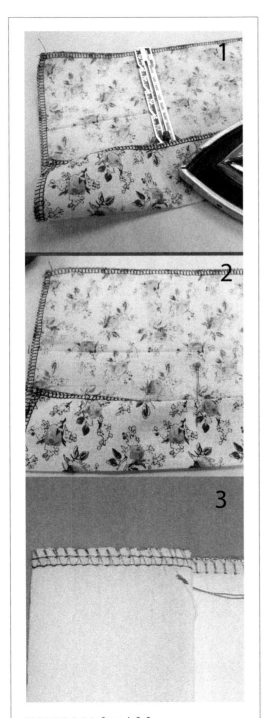

FIGURE 2.24 *Steps 1, 2, 3*

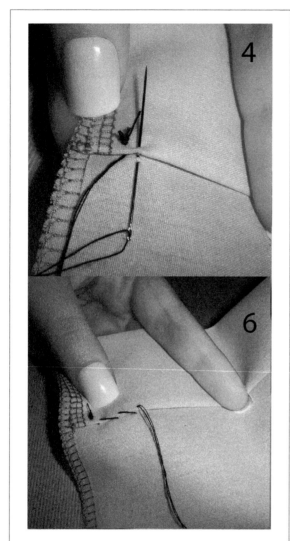

FIGURE 2.25 Steps 4, 6

4. With the needle, grab a few treads of the garment AND a few threads from the top of the hem allowance's fold

    a. Experiment with the hold you use on the fabric and needle. I place the hem on my left, perpendicular to my body and I hold the needle at a 90° angle to the hem.

5. Draw the needle and thread through the stitch
6. Advance about ¼"
7. Repeat steps 4–6 for each stitch, working across the folded edge of the hem allowance

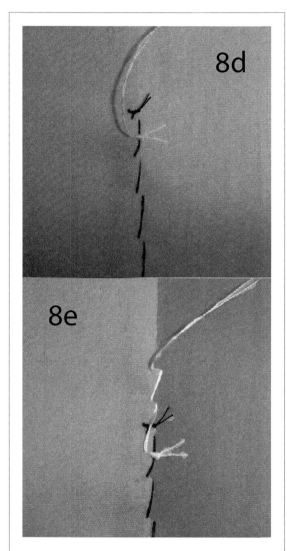

FIGURE 2.26 *Steps 8d, 8e*

8. Running out of thread is very likely. Use this process when the thread on the needle is getting short:
   a. Knot your thread when you have about 4″ remaining past the needle
   b. Less thread will increase the difficulty of creating the knot
   c. Always bury the knot and trim the threads closely
   d. Begin with the next threaded needle and back up a stitch or two so that the beginning of this thread overlaps with the last set of stitches
   e. Continue hemming using the steps 4–6
9. Finish the hemming with a buried knot

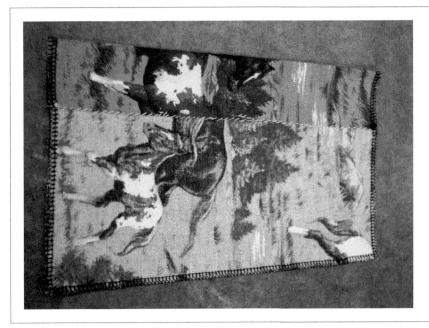

FIGURE 2.27 Sewing Sample #3 finished

Slip Stitch

Hemming with a slip stitch creates a beautiful finish on the garment, inside and outside. It is not, however, fast. This is a two-stroke stitch, and some of the stitching is by feel, not sight.

Sewing Sample #4. Slip Stitch

Figure 2.28 is an enlarged view of the stitching pattern for this hem. The darker lines indicate stitches hidden in the fold. The light-gray lines represent small stitches through the garment layer.

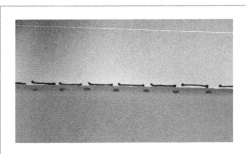

FIGURE 2.28 *Enlarged stitching pattern*

The following steps describe the mechanics of the slip stitch (see Figures 2.29 and 2.30):

1. Simulate a hem to slip stitch by taking one rectangle and folding it up 2" on the 10" length toward the wrong side of the fabric. Just like the whip stitch, this sample has a 2" hem allowance
2. Create another fold that tucks in the overlocked edge of the hem allowance
3. Stitch with the threaded needle facing your recessive hand
4. Place the first stitch on the hem allowance to anchor the knot
5. Take a tiny stitch through the garment layer just above where the hem allowance hits the garment (working from the inside of the fabric)
6. At the same place where that tiny stitch ended, stitch into the fold
7. Travel ¼" *in the fold* and pop out the needle from the fold

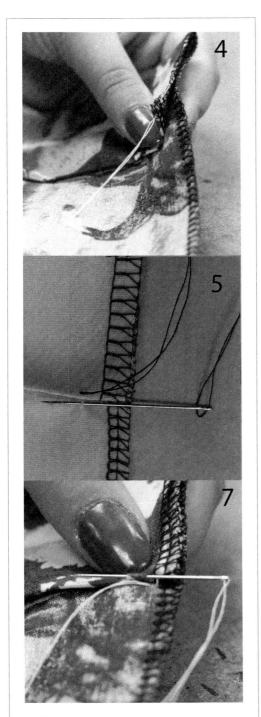

FIGURE 2.29 *Steps 4, 5, 7*

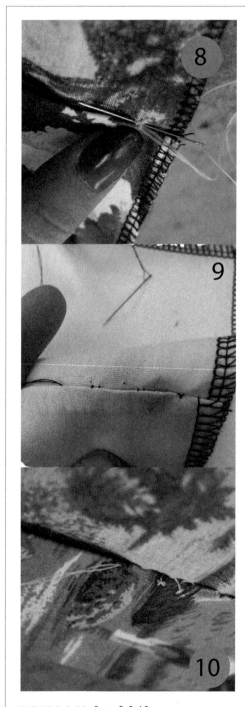

FIGURE 2.30 *Steps 8, 9, 10*

8. Take a tiny stitch through the garment layer just above the location of the stitch that exited the fold
9. Repeat this two-stroke stitch combination until the hemming is finished
10. Running out of thread is very likely. The sub-directions on step 8 of the whip stitch describe the switch to a newly threaded needle
11. Finish the hemming with a buried knot tied on the hem allowance

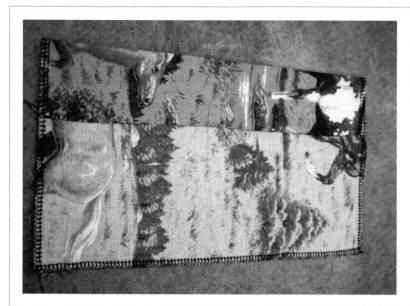

Set aside Sewing Samples #3 and #4 for placement into your portfolio.

FIGURE 2.31 *Sewing Sample #4 finished*

REVIEW

- Describe the orientation of a skirt hook to the finished edge of the garment.
- Name the two parts of a snap.
- What are some of the factors to consider when selecting the correct size snap?
- Which hemming stitch is nearly invisible from the right and wrong side of the fabric?
- When is it best to use the whip stitch to hem a costume?

CHAPTER 3

HOUR SIX

In this chapter, the sewing samples are more complex. Using a sewing machine, iron, and scissors in concert, these exercises will continue to build the skills needed for costume construction.

NECESSARY SUPPLIES FOR CHAPTER 3*

Sewing machine

Sewing machine manual

Tailor's ham

Tracing paper

Tracing wheel

Point turner

10" of single fold bias tape

*Plus previously introduced supplies

INTRODUCTION TO SEWING MACHINES

Dating back to 1755, the first sewing machine was very rudimentary. Today's version is a brilliant combination of complex functions and a simplistic interface. Surprisingly, modern sewing machines of different brands have very similar qualities. Although this book references Bernina sewing machines, other machines will have the same parts in the same places. To jump-start the process of understanding your machine, this section introduces some key terms that reference parts of a sewing machine.

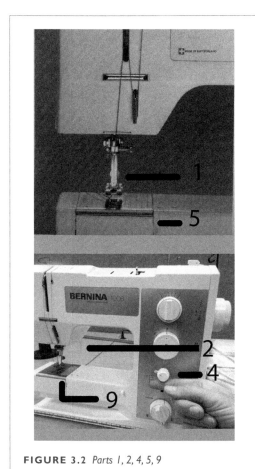

FIGURE 3.2 Parts 1, 2, 4, 5, 9
Credit: Courtesy of Bernina International AG

FIGURE 3.3 Parts 3, 6, 7, 8
Credit: Courtesy of Bernina International AG

Sewing Machine Parts (Figures 3.2 and 3.3 correspond to the following list):

1. Presser foot
2. Presser foot up/down lever
3. Foot pedal
4. Reverse lever
5. Bobbin door
6. Balance wheel
7. Bobbin casing taken out of machine
8. Bobbin
9. Seam allowance guidelines on throat plate

Threading the Sewing Machine

Many machines have similar structural features, yet it is best to refer to the manufacturer's guidelines about threading your machine. A malfunctioning machine may create loose stitches, thread knots, snapped threads, or jammed fabric. Just like a computer re-boot, rethreading your sewing machine solves most problems. Compare the similarities and differences in machines as your experience grows. See Figure 3.4 for an example of threading a machine.

> ### PRO TIP
>
> The Bernina 1006 or 1008 machines are the costume shop standard. No matter which brand you choose, commit to learning that machine. I had a student who worked in my shop for two years, and when she applied at Universal Studios' Costume Shop, her ability to thread their machines, based on her own experience, set her apart from other candidates.

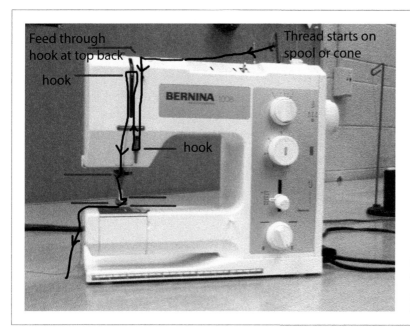

FIGURE 3.4 Threading diagram

Credit: Courtesy of Bernina International AG

MACHINE STITCHING PROJECTS

To build your skills with the sewing machine, Sewing Sample #5–Sample #11 cover basic seams. While each project offers a new challenge, some steps repeat. As the directions allow, the steps combine and are referenced in common sewing vernacular without the previously stated details. Review earlier explanations if necessary.

Sewing the Straight Stitch Seam

Garment construction is rarely without curves; yet here we isolate the straight stitch seam to build familiarity with the machine.

FIGURE 3.5 *Steps 1, 2, 4/5*

Sewing Sample #5. Straight Stitch

The straight stitch project uses two 8″ × 10″ rectangles (see Figures 3.5 and 3.6):

1. Place right sides of fabric together
2. Use straight pins if needed to hold one 10″ edge together
    a. The machine's needle could break if it hits a pin. The flying pieces of the broken needle are dangerous
        i. Prevent injury by placing the heads of the pins on the right, hanging off of the fabric, and remove the pins from the fabric as you sew near them
3. Power on the threaded sewing machine and lift the presser foot
    a. The overlock operates with the foot down and catches the fabric, but the sewing machine requires fabric under the foot prior to sewing. Never engage the foot pedal of the sewing machine without fabric under the presser foot because it will cause the machine to malfunction and unthread
4. Place the fabric's edge 5⁄8″ to the right of the needle
    a. The distance from the stitching to the raw edge of fabric

FIGURE 3.6 *Steps 6, 8*

is the *seam allowance*. The standard seam allowance on manufactured patterns (Simplicity, Butterick, McCall's, and Vogue) is ⅝"; to maintain consistency all of the seams described in this book are ⅝"

b. Sewing machines have various lines on the *throat plate* that indicate different seam allowances. Often stitchers place a piece of tape at the ⅝" line to highlight it

5. Begin with about an inch of fabric under the presser foot

   a. The measurement does not have to be exact

   b. The edge of the fabric layers should be stacked on top of each other

6. Lower the presser foot

7. Hold the thread from the needle with the left hand while cranking the balance wheel until the needle is in the fabric

   a. Operate the balance wheel by cranking down and toward you. Operating in the other direction will knot or break the thread

8. Release the thread

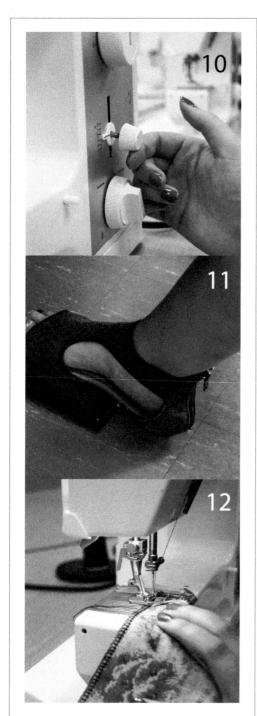

FIGURE 3.7 *Steps 10, 11, 12*

Steps 10–14 describe the technique of *backstitching*. Backstitching locks seams to prevent them from pulling apart (see Figures 3.7 and 3.8).

9. Move your right hand away from the balance wheel and to the reverse button/lever
10. Press or pull up on the reverse lever (operation may vary slightly among different machines)
11. Carefully press the foot pedal and stitch to the back edge of the rectangles
12. Stop sewing at the end of the fabric
    a. Remember that the sewing machine cannot operate properly without fabric under the foot
    b. The speed of the machine is managed by the pressure you place on the foot pedal
13. Release the reverse lever/button

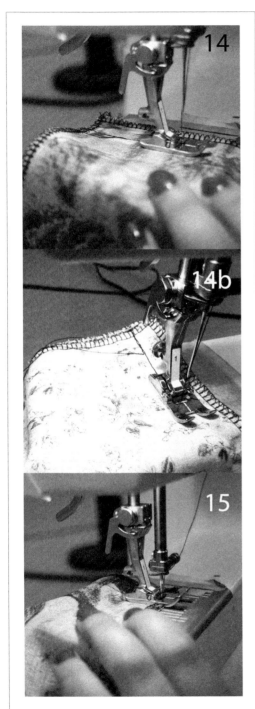

FIGURE 3.8 *Steps 14, 14b, 15*

14. Press the foot pedal to sew forward
    a. Manage the speed with your foot
    b. Check to keep the fabric layers stacked on top of each other
    c. Monitor the edge of the fabric to match with the seam allowance guideline on the throat plate
15. Stop at the opposite edge of the rectangle

FIGURE 3.9 *Steps 16, 17, 20*

Backstitch at the beginning **and** end of the seam. Steps 16–19 describe finishing a seam with backstitching (see Figures 3.9 and 3.10).

16. Engage the reverse lever/button
17. Press the foot pedal to sew in reverse for about 1″
18. Use the balance wheel (always cranking down and toward you) to raise the needle to its highest position
19. Lift the presser foot
20. Pull the fabric away from the machine – roughly one foot
    a. Leave the long threads hanging from the machine. This length keeps the machine threaded. On your next seam, hold these threads while putting the needle into the fabric (step 8 in this sequence)

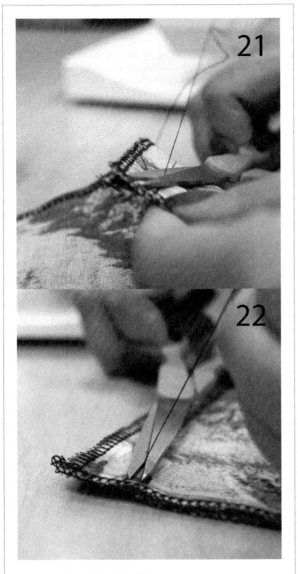

FIGURE 3.10 *Steps 21, 22*

21. Trim the threads between the machine and the fabric at the edge of the fabric
22. Trim the threads that are from the start of the seam. Try to combine the two thread trimming actions without putting down the scissors.

FIGURE 3.11 Steps 23, 24, 25

Quality sewing incorporates frequent ironing during the construction process. Steps 24–26 specify the technique of ironing a finished seam (see Figure 3.11).

23. Place the fabric right side down on the ironing surface
24. Iron the seam allowances open and splay them opposite each other
25. Place the fabric right side up and iron the piece a second time to ensure the removal of wrinkles

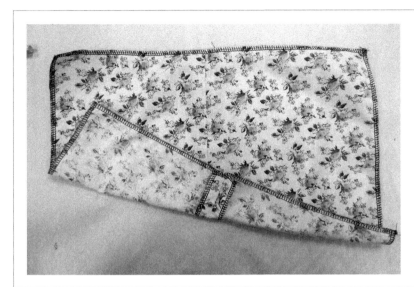

This is an example of your first completed machine stitching sample. Set it aside for placement into the portfolio.

FIGURE 3.12 *Sewing Sample #5 finished*

Straight Stitch Seam With Top Stitching

Top stitching is a great way to add detail to a garment. It can also reduce the bulk of a seam allowance or dictate a garment's fold. Do your jeans have any top stitching? Is it decorative, functional, or both?

FIGURE 3.13 *Steps 2a (top stitching done with the wrong side of the fabric facing up), 2a (top stitching done with the right side of the fabric facing up), 3e*

Sewing Sample #6. Straight Stitch With Top Stitching

These steps begin by creating another straight stitch sample and adding top stitching onto it (see Figures 3.13–3.15).

1. With two 8″ × 10″ rectangles, begin by doing a straight stitch seam just like Sewing Sample #5.
   a. By repeating the straight stitch seam for this project, the technique becomes more familiar
2. Use the width of the presser foot as your seam allowance indicator by lining up the edge of the presser foot against the stitching from the straight stitch
   a. Work the top stitching with either the right *or* wrong side of the fabric facing up
3. Start with backstitching
   a. Place the fabric about 1″ under the presser foot
   b. Lower the presser foot
   c. Hold the thread with your left hand
   d. Crank the balance wheel until the needle is in the fabric
   e. Release the thread
   f. Move your right hand from the balance wheel to the reverse lever

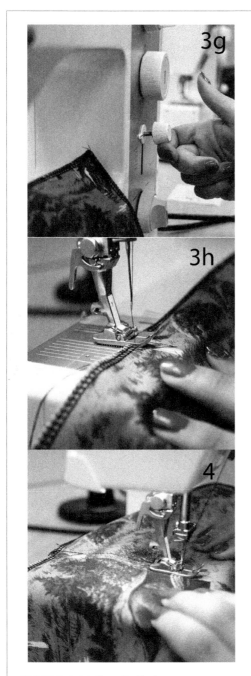

FIGURE 3.14 *Steps 3g, 3h, 4*

g. Engage the reverse
h. Press the foot pedal until the stitching reaches the back of the fabric
i. Release the reverse

4. Advance the fabric to the edge

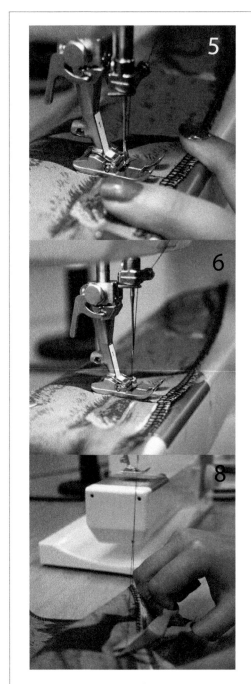

FIGURE 3.15 Steps 5, 6, 8

5. Backstitch to lock the end of the seam
6. Raise the needle
7. Raise the presser foot
8. Trim the threads
9. Repeat the process to top stitch on the other side of the seam to create a second row of top stitching

Finish your sewing by ironing. Set aside for your portfolio.

FIGURE 3.16 *Sewing Sample #6 finished*

HOUR SEVEN

CURVED SEAMS

Common to costume construction are curved seams. Sewing Samples #7 and #8 practice two types of curves and the proper finishing of these stitches. Begin with concave curves that are thinner at the center than at the edges. Next, convex curves widen at the middle and remain thin at the edges. Here is a mnemonic device that might help: con*cave* curves look like a *cave*'s entrance and con*vex* curves have *flex*ed in the middle to look bigger.

FIGURE 3.17 Steps 2, 3, 4

The next two projects begin with a pair of 8″ × 10″ rectangles. Create curves following these directions (see Figure 3.17):

1. Place the two rectangles with right sides together, matching all edges
2. With chalk, draw an arch
   a. Begin on the 8″ side and draw through the center of the rectangle and finishing at the opposite 8″ side
   b. The mark should not get too close to the top or bottom (10″ side) of the rectangle
3. Using scissors, cut along the mark
4. Set aside the convex pair (wider in the middle of the arch)

Concave Curve

Most frequently seen on the neck edge, concave curves are often a part of costume construction.

Sewing Sample #7. Concave Curve

The following steps create the seam and finish treatment for the concave curve (see Figures 3.18 and 3.19):

1. Pin the two layers of the concave fabric together at the recently cut edge
2. Start about 1" in from the edge and 5/8" from the side of the fabric
   a. Remove the pins from the fabric as you sew near them
3. Backstitch
   a. The difficulty is increased because there is a curve in this backstitch
   b. Maintain the 5/8" seam allowance

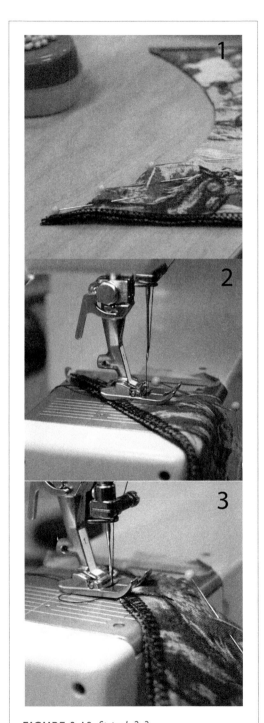

FIGURE 3.18 *Steps 1, 2, 3*

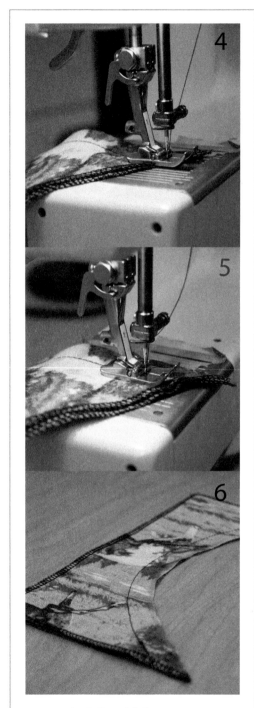

FIGURE 3.19 *Steps 4, 5, 6*

4. Sew forward to the end
   a. Regulate the speed with the foot pedal to accommodate turning the fabric as needed to keep the seam allowance consistent at ⅝"
5. Backstitch
6. Remove the fabric from the machine and trim threads

FIGURE 3.20 Steps 7, 7a

After turning the fabric to the right side, ironing the seam now will create a lumpy and uneven curve. The curve seams need specific treatment of the seam allowance prior to pressing.

Manage the seam allowance with these two steps (see Figures 3.20 and 3.21):

7. *Grading the seam* (allowance) in the following manner will dissipate the bulk of seam allowance and it will gradually disappear

   a. Use scissors and cut down one layer of seam allowance to half of its original width. One layer is trimmed at ¼″ and the second layer is still ⅝″, thus making the seam allowance less bulky

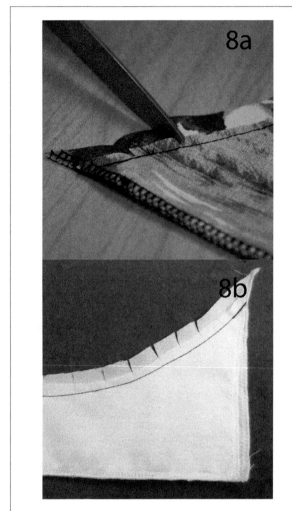

FIGURE 3.21 *Steps 8a, 8b*

8. *Clipping the seam* (allowance) in the following manner allows the fabric to splay/stretch enough to lay flat when ironed.
    a. At about 1" intervals, cut small slits into the seam allowance
    b. Cut through the shorter and longer layers of the seam allowance but do not cut through the stitching. It will create a hole in the seam
9. Turn the fabric to show the right side on the outside
10. Iron carefully along the seam, alternating from the inside and outside until the sample lays flat along the seam .

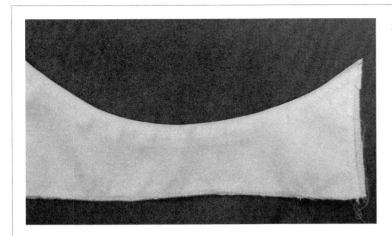

Add Sewing Sample #7 to the portfolio.

FIGURE 3.22 *Sewing Sample #7 finished*

Convex Curve

Convex curves are on rounded collars, scalloped edges, and anywhere the costume designer has designated.

Sewing Sample #8. Convex Curve

This project uses the remaining pair of curves that were set aside in the previous sequence (step 3).

FIGURE 3.23 *Steps 1, 2, 4*

Many but not all of the steps for this curve have been introduced. As you follow along, what stands out as new? Use Figure 3.23 as a reference.

1. Pin the two layers of the convex fabric together at the recently cut edge with right sides together
2. Start about 1" in from the edge and 5/8" from the side of the fabric
   a. Remove the pins from the fabric as you sew near them
3. Backstitch
   a. There may be a little of a curve to this backstitch
   b. Maintain the 5/8" seam allowance
4. Sew forward to the end
   a. Regulate the speed with the foot pedal to accommodate turning the fabric as needed to keep the seam allowance consistent at 5/8"
5. Backstitch
6. Remove the fabric from the machine and trim threads

FIGURE 3.24 *Steps 7a, 7bi, 7bii*

Again, ironing the seam now will not yield a desired result. Use the following steps to create a finished look on the curved seam (see Figure 3.24).

7. Manage the seam allowance prior to turning and ironing with these two steps:
    a. Grading the seam (allowance) thus making the seam allowance gradually disappear
    b. *Notching the seam* (allowance) allows the fabric to condense and lay flat when ironed
        i. At about 1" intervals, cut small V shapes out of the seam allowance. Cut the wide part of the V on the raw edge and the cut lines come together just above the stitching. Don't cut past the stitching line.
        ii. Cut through the shorter and longer layers of the seam allowance
8. Turn the fabric to the right side
9. Iron carefully along the seam
    a. Alternate ironing from the inside and outside until the project lays flat along the seam

Sewing Sample #8 is ready for the portfolio.

FIGURE 3.25 *Sewing Sample #8 finished*

PRO TIP

Once a seam is graded, clipped, or notched, letting out the seam allowance for expansion is nearly impossible. When working in a costume shop, always verify with the pattern maker or shop manager prior to cutting into or off seam allowance.

90° Corner

Points, even those not exactly 90°, are common to costume construction and sewn with the same steps and treatments described here.

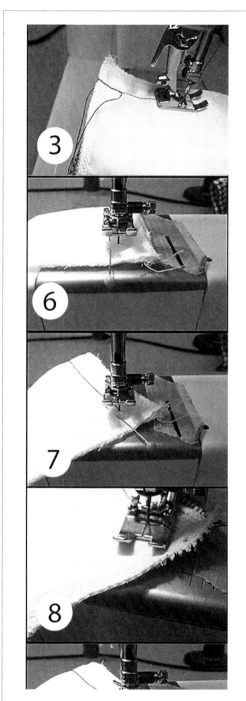

FIGURE 3.26 *Steps 3, 6, 7, 8 correspond to the 90° corner*

Sewing Sample #9. 90° Corner

The following steps are the same as a straight stitch except for the very specific pivot (see Figures 3.26–3.27).

1. Begin with two rectangles placed right sides together
2. (Optional) Pin along one 10″ side and an adjoining 8″
3. Start the seam along either edge. Backstitch
4. Continue forward

This section describes the two 45° pivots that combine to create the 90° corner:

5. ⅝″ shy of the corner, stop while the needle is in the fabric
    a. If necessary, use the balance wheel to put the needle into the fabric
6. Raise the presser foot
7. Pivot the fabric 45° (not 90°)
8. Place the presser foot back down

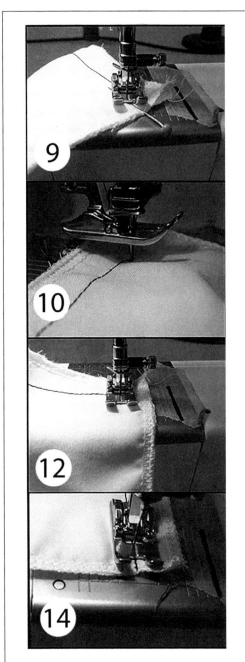

FIGURE 3.27 *Steps 9, 10, 12, 14 correspond to the 90° corner*

9. Make one stitch
   a. Since this is difficult to do, use the balance wheel and crank one cycle to create the stitch
10. Raise the presser foot
11. Pivot the fabric 45° for the second time
12. Place the presser foot back down
13. Finish the seam to the end of the second side
14. Backstitch
15. Remove the fabric from the machine

16. Trim threads

Just like the concave and convex curves, make adjustments to the seam allowance of the 90° corner prior to turning and ironing.

These directions will mitigate the bulky seam allowance at the point. When possible, the steps are abbreviated if they were previously introduced (see Figure 3.28).

17. Grade the seam allowance on both the 8″ and the 10″ edges
18. Cut off the seam allowance parallel to the 45° stitch
19. Cut off the edges right and left of the previous cut
20. Carefully turn the right side of the fabric to the outside

FIGURE 3.28 *Steps 17, 18, 19*

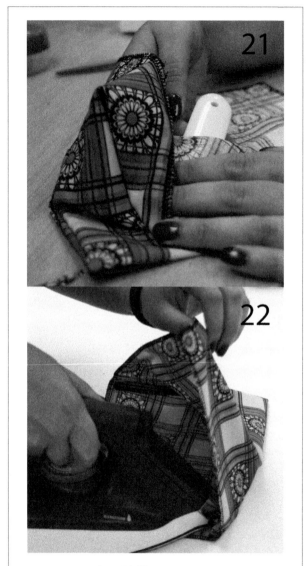

FIGURE 3.29 Steps 21, 22

21. Using a *point turner* from the inside (wrong side) of the fabric, gently push the corner (see Figure 3.29)
    a. This step creates the desired sharp finish for the corner
    b. Caution: A scissor's tip, a pencil, and a seam ripper might all appear to be tools adequate to turn a corner, yet they pop through the seam, causing a hole in the garment. Even a point turner requires gentle use because of the very narrow seam allowance at the corner
22. Iron the finished sewing sample

Set aside Sewing Sample #9 for the portfolio.

FIGURE 3.30 *Sewing Sample #9 finished*

HOUR EIGHT

DART

Darts are triangle-shaped seams that remove fabric and tighten the garment's fit. Think of a globe sliced and displayed on a flat surface (see Figure 3.31). Take those triangle-shaped voids and sew them up; the map returns to a globe. In that analogy, the body is a sphere, fabric is flat, and to mold the fabric to the body, you can use darts to create a rounded shape.

FIGURE 3.31 *Drawing of a globe sliced to lay flat. The sliced pieces are similar to darts in a garment*

Sewing Sample #10. Dart

Exact shapes and sizes of darts vary widely in costume construction because the needs of the garment are never the same. Designers can add lines and detail to the costume with various darts. They can even be specific to a fashion trend and associated with an historical era.

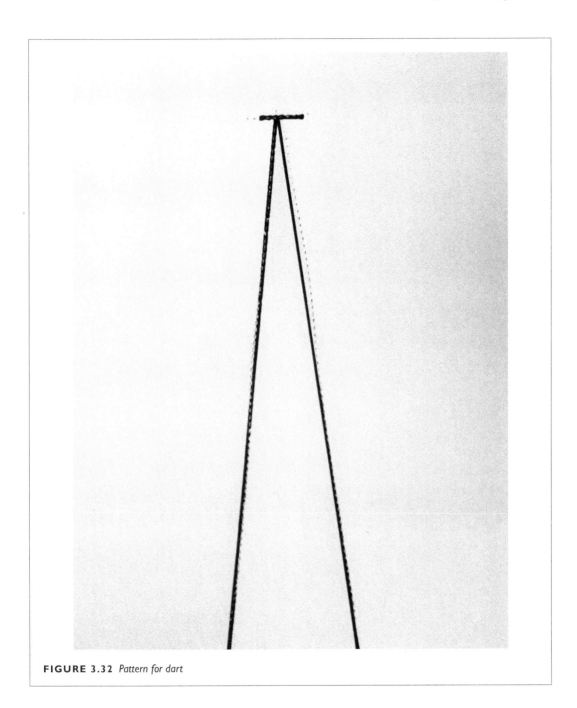

FIGURE 3.32 *Pattern for dart*

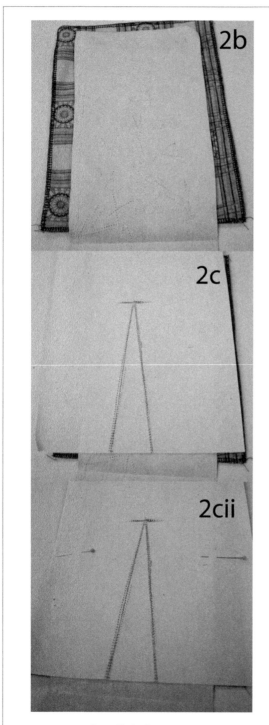

FIGURE 3.33 Steps 2b, 2c, 2cii

This exercise replicates a simple dart from a commercial pattern (see Figures 3.33 and 3.34).

1. Trace the dart pattern from this book (see Figure 3.32) to a sheet of paper
2. Use the following subset of instructions to transfer the dart's lines to the wrong side of an 8″ × 10″ fabric rectangle
   a. Place the fabric wrong side up on the table
   b. With the ink side to the wrong side, put the *tracing paper* on top of the fabric
   c. Set the pattern piece on top of the tracing paper
      i. The wide part of the dart pattern is on the 8″ side of the rectangle
      ii. Hold or pin the layers together

d. Using a *tracing wheel*, follow the pattern's lines and transfer the marks to the wrong side of the fabric
e. Unstack the pattern, tracing paper, and fabric

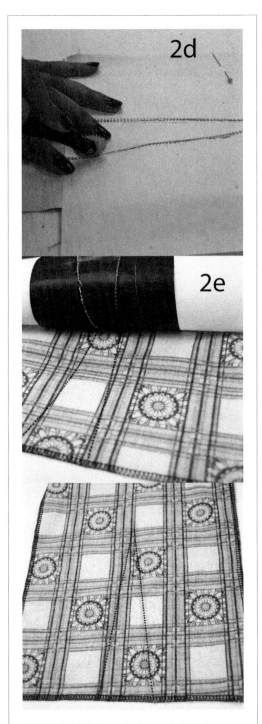

FIGURE 3.34 *Steps 2d, 2e, marked fabric*

The machine is used a little differently when stitching the dart (see Figure 3.35).

3. Fold the fabric with the right sides together in an orientation that begins to put one edge of the mark on top of the other mark
4. Pin the two lines on top of each other
   a. For accuracy, pin into the top layer and check to see if the pin exited the lower layer at the marked line
   b. It is helpful to put the points of the pins facing the wide part of the dart
5. Start your stitching on the marked line, in from the edge of the wide part of the dart
6. Backstitch to the edge
7. Sew forward along the line
   a. Remove the pins as you sew
8. At the tip of the dart, *do not backstitch*. Stitch to the very end of the point
   a. Backstitching at the end of a dart would create a pucker

FIGURE 3.35 *Steps 3, 5, 7a*

These steps describe the finishing treatment of the dart (see Figures 3.36 and 3.37)

9. Stop the machine
10. Raise the needle
11. Raise the presser foot
12. Pull the fabric from the machine
13. Cut the threads leaving at least 6″ hanging off the point of the dart
14. Hand tie a square knot with the thread at the point of the dart
    a. Knotting the threads is an old technique originating from men's tailoring

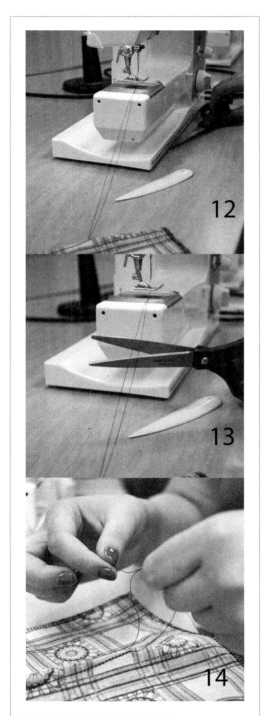

FIGURE 3.36 Steps 12, 13, 14

FIGURE 3.37 Steps 15, 16

15. Trim the knotted threads to 1"
16. Trim the threads at the wide part of the dart where the seam started, close to the fabric as usual

Darts create dimension therefore, ironing against a flat surface is counterproductive. The following instructions step you through the finish (see Figure 3.38).

17. Place the rectangle on a *tailor's ham* wrong side up
    a. Mold the curve of the fabric around the ham
18. Iron the dart to one side
19. Turn the fabric over and iron again

On this exercise, the dart irons to either side. In a practical application, the dart irons to the center of the garment.

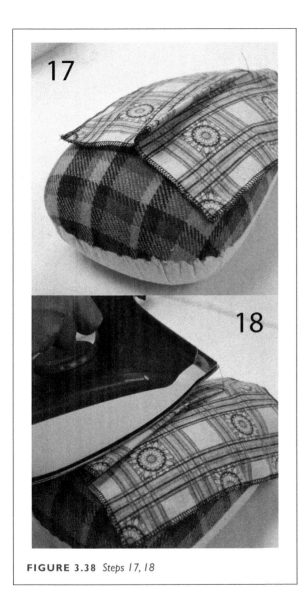

FIGURE 3.38 *Steps 17, 18*

Knowing that the dart won't lay flat will add to the challenge of putting it into your portfolio.

FIGURE 3.39 *Sewing Sample #10 finished*

PRO TIP

Sewing a dart breaks many rules:
- No ⅝" seam allowance, instead you stitch on the transferred line
- No backstitching on the tip of the dart
  - Knot the thread to prevent the seam from unraveling. Trim the threads to 1" after the knot
- The seam allowance is not splayed open
  - Press dart to one side using a tailor's ham

Hemming With Bias Tape

There are times, perhaps too many, when a garment is just long enough to use on stage but not long enough to have any hem allowance. In those instances, use *bias tape* to 'fake' the hem allowance.

As previously mentioned, the bias of the fabric is that which runs 45° from the grain. Bias tape is made from strips of fabric cut on that angle. While it is very convenient to purchase bias tape, the ambitious stitcher can always make their own (not covered in this beginner's book).

FIGURE 3.40 Steps 2, 3, 4

Sewing Sample #11. Hemming With Bias Tape

This sample attaches the tape, simulates hem allowance, and reviews the whip stitch (see Figures 3.39 and 3.40).

1. Place the bias tape's right side to the right side of an 8″ × 10″ rectangle of fabric
   a. Most commercially made bias tape is labeled single fold (and strangely has two folds – double fold has three folds)
2. Open up the fold near the raw edge of the rectangle so that raw edges of the bias tape and the fabric are together
3. Pin if desired
4. Your stitching line is the fold of the bias tape; not ⅝″
5. Backstitch at the beginning and the end
6. Trim threads

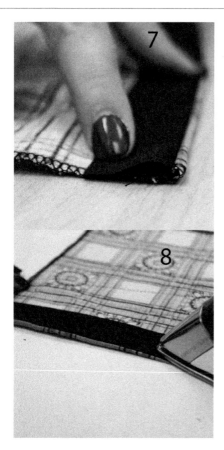

FIGURE 3.41 *Steps 7, 8*

FIGURE 3.42 *Hemming partially completed*

7. Turn the bias tape 360° until the wrong side of the bias tape is against the wrong side of the fabric
8. Iron
   a. Knowing that the right side of the garment faces the audience, ironing should be sharp and the bias tape completely on the wrong side of the garment

Now you have hem allowance, but the edge isn't hemmed. The last steps describe the finish (see Figure 3.42).

9. Whip stitch the top of the bias tape to the rectangle
   a. Use the technique described in the whip stitch exercise
   b. Use the top fold of the bias tape as the tucked-in edge of the hem allowance
10. Iron the front and back of the finished sample

Add this to your portfolio.

FIGURE 3.43 *Sewing Sample #11 finished*

REVIEW

- Rethread the sewing machine. Time yourself on this task. Can you do it in under two minutes?
- Why are seams backstitched?
- Name some uses for top stitching.
- What is *grading the seam*?
- Why are curves clipped or notched?
- Is the concave curve notched or clipped?
- Describe the three cuts needed on the seam allowance at the tip of a 90° corner.

CHAPTER 4

H O U R   N I N E

INTRODUCING THE SCRUB SHIRT

Now, for the application of your newly acquired skill set: the scrub shirt. This will not be your *Mona Lisa*, yet it will be within your abilities. Unlike the preceding projects, the scrub shirt overlaps several hours. Follow along and through to the end.

NECESSARY SUPPLIES FOR CHAPTER 4*

Simplicity Pattern #4101 (it comes in sizes XS–XL and XL–XXXL)

About 2.5 yards of woven fabric
- The measurement from selvage to selvage (width) should be 45″ or more

*Plus previously introduced supplies

Reading a Pattern

Major sewing stores offer thousands of pattern choices. Both the front and back of the pattern contain critical information. The front displays the finished project. The back of the envelope contains technical information. This book steps through Simplicity Pattern #4101 B Top.

The front of the pattern's envelope (see Figure 4.2) entices the shopper while simultaneously containing important information. Look for the following items on the scrub shirt cover:

- Photograph (sometimes a drawing) of the finished garment
- Variations contained within the pattern
- Pattern size or range of sizes

The back of the pattern is an information overload (see Figure 4.3). The following instructions will assist in reading the back of the envelope by breaking it down into smaller units:

1. Begin by eliminating the unnecessary information
    a. Cross out one of the two languages
    b. Cross out all references to D Pants
    c. Eliminate information on A Top and C Top
2. The remaining horizontal sub-sections are outlined below
    a. **WOMEN'S AND MEN'S SCRUB TOPS AND PANTS**
       It seems redundant, but this line clarifies the pattern's content
    b. **Fabrics:** Laundered cotton, baby cord (corduroy), batiks, broadcloth, calico, chambray, lightweight denim, extra fabric to match plaids, stripes, or one-way design fabrics.

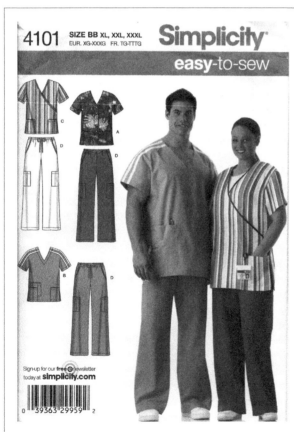

FIGURE 4.2 *Front of pattern envelope*
Credit: Courtesy of Simplicity Patterns

This information indicates the recommended fabrics.

For ease of construction, skip the plaids, stripes, or one-way design fabrics, as they add greatly to the complexity of construction

c. Notions: Thread. **A**: Six ⅝" buttons.

The bold **A** indicates notions for that specific view.

Since we are constructing B Top, buttons are not applicable, but you will need thread

d. BODY MEASUREMENTS

Determine the shirt size using the chest/bust measurement. For example, a chest measuring 50" is a size L (large).

It is always a good idea to know the chest, waist, and hip measurements for the wearer of the garment so that you can buy the correct pattern size. Luckily, most patterns are *nested* with many sizes printed on the same tissue paper. (Note the multiple sizes listed on the front of the pattern.) Although buying a pattern in a bunch of sizes is very convenient, once you start cutting and working with the tissue paper, it won't be useable a second time. The pattern's paper is so thin that cutting away the larger sizes and across smaller sizes equivocates to a one-use purchase.

e. Sizes

The paper pattern pieces do not reference body measurements; sizes are abbreviated XS, S, M, L, XL, XXL, and XXXL

f. B Top

This area lists lengths of fabric needed per size and based on the width of fabric. When buying fabric for costumes prior to knowing the cast, estimate high. Being short on fabric can be a big problem. More information about determining the amount of fabric in step 3

g. Interfacing ½ yd of 22" to 25" lightweight fusible interfacing is a textile used to stiffen fabric. To save money and time, this book completely omits the use of interfacing.

h. A, B, C, Ribbon Ties is optional (opt.) 1⅞ yd of ⅝" wide

This book does not discuss the application of ribbon

i. GARMENT MEASUEMENTS (Bust/Chest & Hip Printed on Pattern Tissue)

This informs the stitcher about the fit of the garment. For example, in this section the chart shows that a size XL garment measures

61″ when finished. The BODY MEASUREMENT section indicated that an XL garment fits a person with a 52″ chest. This means the shirt is 9″ bigger than the wearer. It is correct to conclude that these tops have a loose fit.

If you are between sizes or desire a closer fit, build a shirt one size smaller than suggested.

The difference between the body measurement and the garment measurement is called *ease*.

3. To determine the amount of required fabric, intersect the vertical **size** column and the horizontal row B Top (lower section of Figure 4.3)

   a. There are two numbers at the intersection. One length references fabric 45″ wide and the other 60″

   To determine the width of your chosen fabric, check for a sticker on the end of the cardboard bolt or measure from selvage to selvage. Use the horizontal line specific to the width of your fabric that intersects with the correct size. For example, purchase 2⅝ yards if the fabric is 45″ wide; purchase 1⅝ yards of 60″ fabric for a size large.

> **PRO TIP**
>
> Sixty-inch-wide fabric requires a shorter length to create the scrub shirt. This sounds economical, yet wider fabric is often more expensive. Consider the time to construct the garment as a commodity too. Buy fabric that inspires creativity over price. Use sales and coupons to save money rather than making compromises.

Laying Out and Cutting the Shirt

Use a large surface for laying out the fabric. In a home, the floor or a dining table could provide enough surface area. Be careful about lower surfaces because prolonged crouching or hunching can cause back pain. In the costume shop, a cutting table works perfectly. Here are the steps for laying out and cutting out the scrub shirt (see Figures 4.4–4.9):

Chapter 4 Hour Nine 103

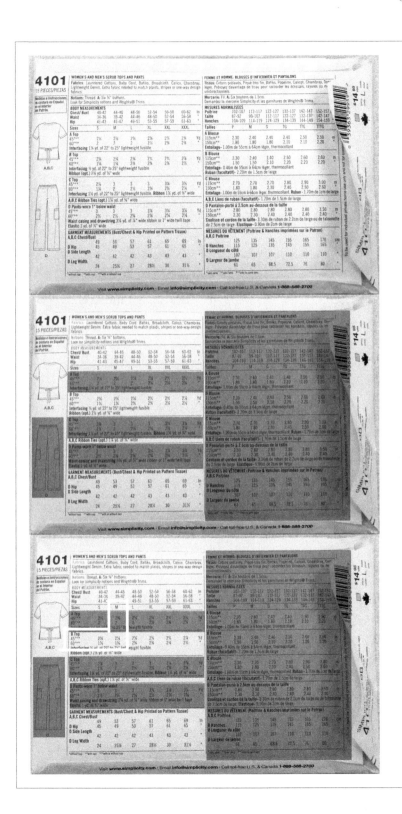

FIGURE 4.3 Back of pattern envelope. Unnecessary information is grayed out

Credit: Courtesy of Simplicity Patterns

FIGURE 4.4 *Five pattern pieces needed to build the scrub shirt*

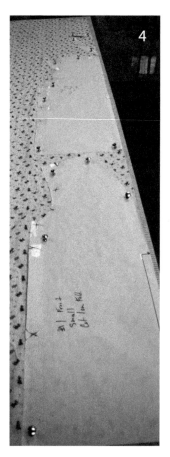

FIGURE 4.5 *Place the four cut-on-the-fold pieces first*

1. Open the envelope and locate the five pattern pieces needed for B Top
   a. Front
   b. Back
   c. Front facing
   d. Back facing
   e. Sleeve
2. Roughly cut out the five pattern pieces – set aside
3. With wrong sides together, fold the fabric down the length
   a. This puts the selvage edges on top of each other
   b. The fold is parallel to the selvage. Therefore, the fold is on the grain
   c. When the wrong side of the fabric is together, transferring marks is easier
4. Pin the four pieces indicating the fold against the fabric's fold (see Figure 4.5)
   a. Placing pattern pieces upside down is allowed

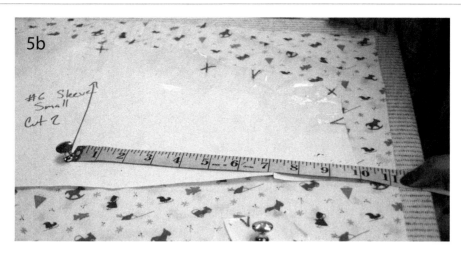

FIGURE 4.6 *Align the sleeve with the grain. For clarity, the size small was traced from the tissue pattern piece*

5. Place the last piece, the sleeve, *on the grain* of the fabric. Accurately aligning the grain prevents the fabric from twisting around the body

a. Pin the pattern to the fabric at one end of the double-arrow line

b. Measure the distance from the pinned end to the selvage – note that distance

FIGURE 4.7 *Measure the opposite end of the double arrow and adjust to make the line parallel to the selvage*

c. Toward the other end of the sleeve, measure up from the selvage the same amount

d. Pivot the pattern until the distance is the same from each side of the double-arrowed line to the selvage

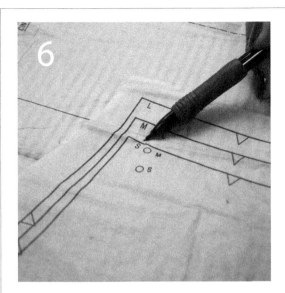

FIGURE 4.8 *Referring to the tissue pattern pieces, cut on the line indicating the desired size*

FIGURE 4.9 *Never cut open or cut through the folded edge of the fabric*

6. Using a sharp scissors, cut on the bold lines indicating your desired size

   a. Cut only around the outer edge of each piece. Do not cut open the fold

   b. The triangles that protrude past the cutting line are *notches*. The notches help with the accuracy of project assembly

      i. If the notches protrude, cut them off. (You can still see the location because the notches are also indicated to the inside of the cutting line) – this is revisited in step 7

   c. Leave the pieces on your flat surface after cutting

Using tracing paper and a tracing wheel, mark the notches and circles located on the parameter of each pattern piece. The following directions outline the process (see Figures 4.10–4.12)

7. Fold the tracing paper in half with un-inked sides together. Now it marks the top and bottom of the fabric with one stroke. Slide the marking paper between the two layers of fabric. Shift the marking paper around the perimeter of each piece as needed. Keep the marks within ⅝" of the edge to prevent them from showing on the finished garment. Circles are difficult to trace; instead, make an X with the two lines intersecting at the center of the circle.

FIGURE 4.10 *Note the way the pattern, fabric, and marking paper are placed*

FIGURE 4.11 *Marking the notches*

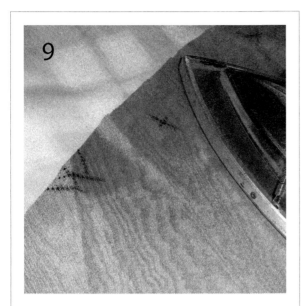

FIGURE 4.12 *Iron all of the cut pieces*

8. Clean up the cutting area
   a. Set aside the pattern pieces
   b. Put away the tracing paper and tracing wheel
9. Open up, separate, and iron the fabric pieces

HOUR TEN

CONSTRUCTING THE SHIRT

Both experienced and novice stitchers make mistakes. Be patient with the learning process. Removing stitches with a seam ripper is fast and easy. I often joke that I'm not a better sewer, I just fix my mistakes quickly.

Overlock

Prevent fraying by overlocking every edge of the garment (see Figure 4.13).

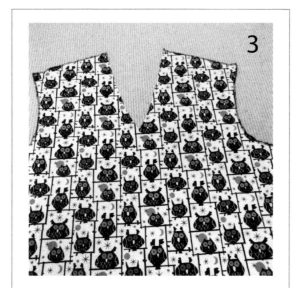

FIGURE 4.13 *Sharp inside corner of front piece and front facing piece is not overlocked*

1. Make sure that the pieces have been unfolded
   a. Overlock only single layers of fabric
2. Keep the square edges squared
3. Do not overlock the V-shaped neck edge on the front piece or the V-shaped neck edge on the front neck facing
   a. The corner is too sharp, and the chopping blade could gouge into the fabric

Stitch Shoulder Seams

Look at the front and back pieces. Identify the neck edge, armholes, side seams, and the shoulder seams (see Figures 4.14 and 4.15).

Back at the sewing machine, the first step of the scrub shirt will be similar to the straight stitch seam done on the rectangle fabric (Sewing Sample #5).

1. With right sides together, stitch the front to back at shoulders
   a. This pattern is about ½" longer on the back shoulder seam compared to the front shoulder seam. This extra fabric allows for the shoulder curve
   b. Stretch the front shoulder seam to match the back
   c. Use pins if desired
2. Backstitch the beginning and end of the seams
3. Press the seam allowance open

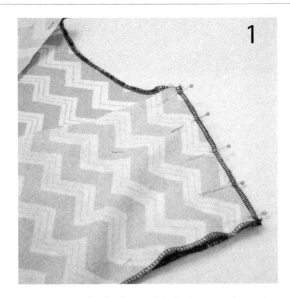

FIGURE 4.14 *Pin the front and back pieces together at the shoulder seam*

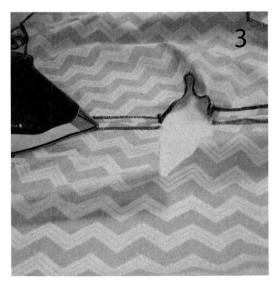

FIGURE 4.15 *Press seam allowances open*

STITCHING SHOULDER SEAMS ON FACINGS

Ultimately, the facing pieces finish the neck edge of the shirt. Prepare the facings as follows (see Figures 4.16 and 4.17):

1. With the right side of the front facing against the right side of the back facing, stitch at the shoulders
2. This tiny seam still needs backstitching at the beginning and end
3. Press the seam allowances open

FIGURE 4.16 *Stitch front and back facings together at shoulder seams*

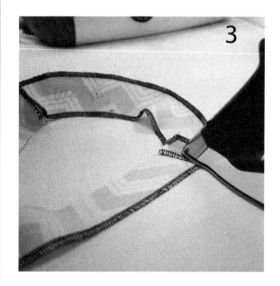

FIGURE 4.17 *Press seam allowances open*

HOUR ELEVEN

FINISHING THE NECK EDGE

The facings attach to the body, creating a finished edge around the neck (see Figures 4.18–4.29).

> **PRO TIP**
>
> Whether stitching the 90° corner or the point at the front of the scrub shirt, tight turns are tricky. To pivot the fabric, raise the presser foot. Turn and then put the presser foot down again for the next stitch; even single stitches done with the balance wheel. The thread will knot while stitching with the presser foot raised.

FIGURE 4.18 *The inner edge of the facings align with the neck edge of the front and back pieces*

1. Open out the front and back body pieces so that they lay somewhat flat. (The garment will not lay completely flat because the seams have started to create the rounded shape of the human form.)
2. With right sides together, place the facing on top of the neck hole
   a. Match raw edges and shoulder seams
   b. Pin

FIGURE 4.19 *Draw the stitching line at the center front*

3. Stitch around the neck edge ⅝" seam allowance. Overlap beginning and ending stitches

   a. The pivot at the tip of the V at the neck is tricky. The garment masks the seam allowance indicator, making the center hard to find

      i. Using chalk and a ruler (or any measuring tool), draw the stitching line by extrapolating ⅝" past the cut edge of the V. Make a line from one side and again from the other side. The intersecting lines specify the pivot point

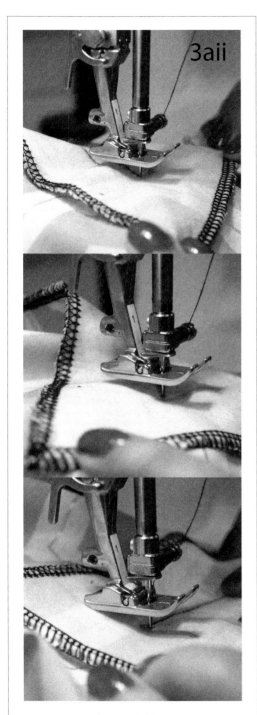

FIGURE 4.20 *Pivot at the V*

ii. Follow this line for a crisp pivot at the center front of the neck

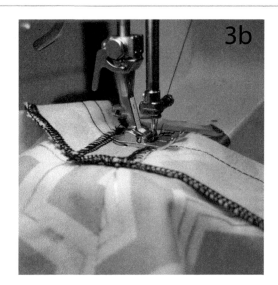

FIGURE 4.21 *Keep seam allowance splayed*

b. When stitching around, keep the seam allowances from the shoulder seams splayed open as you stitch over the layers

FIGURE 4.22 *Grade the seam allowance*

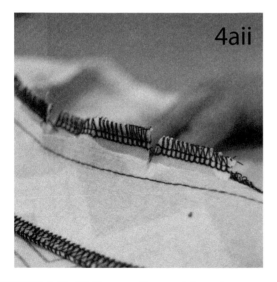

FIGURE 4.23 *Clip the seam allowance at the neck curve*

4. Give the seam allowance special treatment prior to ironing it to the inside of the garment
   a. Grade and clip the seam allowance
      i. Trim one layer of the seam allowance to half the width
      ii. At 1″ intervals, clip the seam allowance on the concave curve at the back of the neck

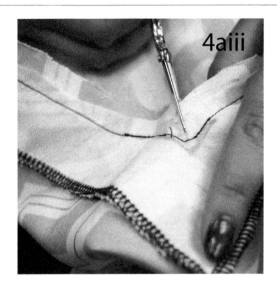

FIGURE 4.24 *Clip once into the V at center front*

FIGURE 4.25 *Good quality construction includes good ironing*

   iii. Make one clip into the seam allowance of the center front V
5. Turn facings to the inside of the garment
6. Iron to create a crease against the seam
   a. Alternate ironing from inside and outside of the garment to complete the crease

7. Pin the facing to the inside of the garment
8. Using a piece of tape, mark on the throat plate 1″ from the sewing machine's needle
9. With a 1″ seam allowance, top stitch around the neck edge

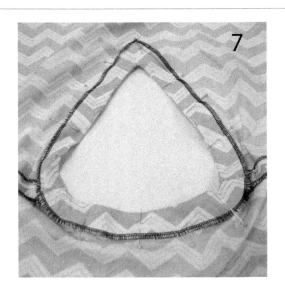

FIGURE 4.26 *Pin perpendicular to the stitching*

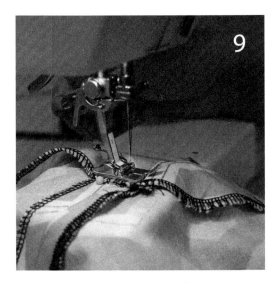

FIGURE 4.27 *The fold aligns with the 1″ mark*

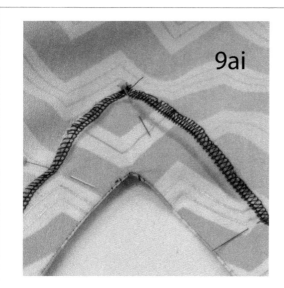

FIGURE 4.28 *Mark the stitching line*

FIGURE 4.29 *Iron the finished neck edge*

a. The pivot at the point of the V is difficult to find because the garment covers up the seam allowance indicator

   i. Using chalk and a ruler, draw the stitching line by extrapolating 1" past the folded edge of the V. Make a line from one side and again from the other side. The intersecting lines specify the pivot point for the V

b. By encasing the raw edge of fabric, it will not fray

10. Iron

HOUR TWELVE

PINNING AND ATTACHING THE SLEEVES

Attaching the sleeves is by far the most challenging part of the shirt's construction (see Figures 4.30–4.34).

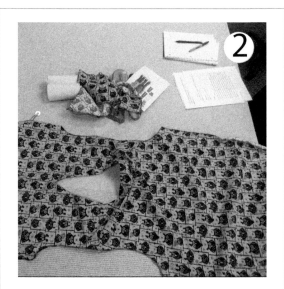

FIGURE 4.30 *Place the garment on the surface as shown*

1. Begin with the body of the shirt open and right side up
2. Place the front of the garment to your left (it will help to make these directions clear)
   a. This means that the left armhole is nearest you

FIGURE 4.31 *Match double notch on sleeve with double notch on back when right sides are together*

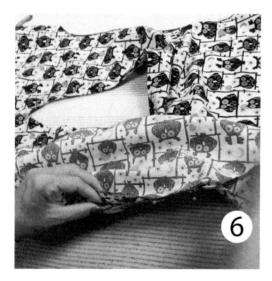

FIGURE 4.32 *Pin sleeve to front and back*

Using the following steps, determine which sleeve will attach to the right and which to the left.

3. On the sleeve, find the double (bigger) notch that indicates the back. The mark is on the wrong side of the fabric, on the rounded side, and near the cut edge
4. With right sides together, align the double notch of the sleeve to the corresponding double notch on the back piece at the armhole edge
5. The concave curve of the armhole is aligned with the convex curve of the top of the sleeve. It will look like these edges will not fit together – they do
6. Match single notches of the sleeve to the armhole. Pin at notches. Pin at 1" intervals. Shift the fabric to match raw edges (the garment will not lay flat)

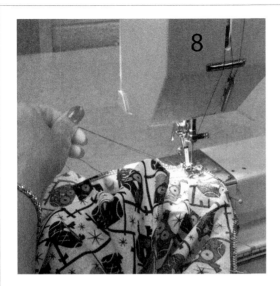

FIGURE 4.33 *Stitching the sleeve*

FIGURE 4.34 *Attach the other sleeve*

7. The sleeve may appear too big for the armhole. Distribute the fullness evenly between all the pins throughout the whole seam
8. Placing the sleeve side down, sew the sleeve to the armhole
   a. When two layers of fabric move through a sewing machine, the lower layer moves through faster. This quirk can be a tool. When one of the layers is longer, like our sleeve, place that layer on the bottom. By the end of the seam, the layers are even because the longer layer traveled faster
9. Repeat the steps to sew the right sleeve to the right armhole
10. It is not necessary to iron this seam

STITCHING SIDE SEAMS

Use one long straight stitch seam to attach the front to the back at the sides and underarm. The seam begins at the edge of the sleeve and ends near the hip at the circle/X mark.

FIGURE 4.35 *Garment with right sides together*

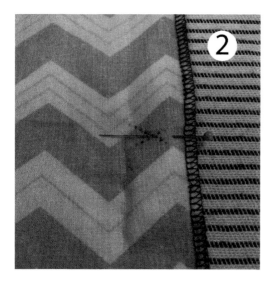

FIGURE 4.36 *Pin the marks together*

Follow the steps to prepare the seam for stitching (see Figures 4.35–4.39):

1. With right sides together, place the front of the garment on top of the bottom
2. Working each side, match the front mark located near the hips to the back mark (these were circles on the paper pattern and transferred to the wrong side of the garment with an X). Pin

3. Pin at the underarm seam
4. Pin all of the seam allowance layers at the sleeve to the sleeve side of that seam
   a. This is different than splaying the seam allowance

FIGURE 4.37 Pin matching the seam lines

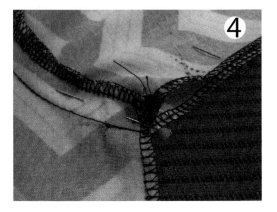

FIGURE 4.38 Add another pin to hold the seam allowance toward the sleeve (not splayed open)

FIGURE 4.39 *Pin from mark to the end of the sleeve*

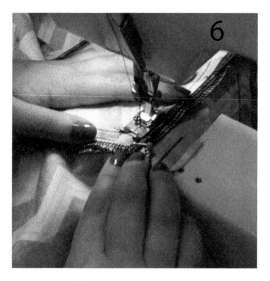

FIGURE 4.40 *Stitch over the underarm seam*

5. Pin from the edge of the sleeve to the underarm and the underarm to the marks at the vent

Closing the sides is almost a straight stitch seam (see Figure 4.40):

6. Sew from the marks through the underarm to the sleeve hem

FIGURE 4.41 *Use a sleeve board to iron the sides and sleeve*

FIGURE 4.42 *Ready the seam allowance of the vent for hemming*

Here are some specific ironing directions that finish this seam and prepare the side *vents* (the open area below the side seam) for hemming (see Figures 4.41 and 4.42):

7. Iron the seam allowance open using a *sleeve board* (narrow ironing boards that slide into garments and allow for pressing sleeves)
8. On the sides, below the seam, iron the edge ⅝" to the wrong side
   a. Pressing back the edges of the vents simplifies the upcoming stitching
9. Repeat the steps needed to sew and iron the other side seam

HOUR THIRTEEN

HEMMING THE SLEEVES

Hemming creates an edge of a garment that finishes on the fold (see Figure 4.43). The directions for the sleeve are similar to the whip stitch 8″ × 10″ rectangle (Sewing Sample #3).

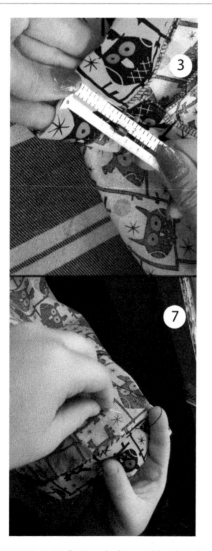

FIGURE 4.43 *Prepare the hem and hand stitch*

1. The pattern allows a 1½″ hem on the sleeves
2. Turn the shirt wrong side out
3. Use a seam gauge to turn 1½″ of the sleeve edge to the wrong side
4. Iron on the fold to create a crisp edge
5. Tuck in the overlocked edge so that it doesn't show
6. Pin to hold the hem allowance
7. Hand stitch the hem with a whip stitch
8. Iron when finished
9. Hem the other sleeve

Shirttail Hemming the Bottom

The finish on the bottom of the shirt is a narrow hem created with two folds. In an exception to the rules, ironing and pinning prior to the hemming is not beneficial (see Figures 4.44–4.46).

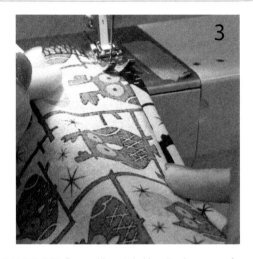

FIGURE 4.44 *Prepped hem is held under the presser foot*

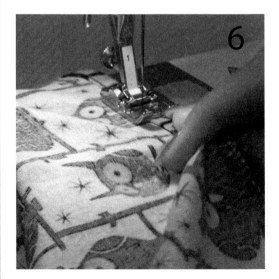

FIGURE 4.45 *Stitch near inside edge*

1. Begin on the front or back – both pieces are hemmed
    a. Start with the wrong side of the fabric up and the creased edge of the side vent unfolded
2. Turn the overlocked edge to the wrong side of the fabric. Then turn those two layers a second time to the wrong side of the fabric
3. Once an inch of fabric is twice turned, put it into the sewing machine
4. Place the presser foot down, hold the thread, and crank the balance wheel to insert the needle
5. Backstitch
    a. Stitch near the fold of the inside edge
6. Sew forward to the end, keeping the stitching near the fold of the inside edge

FIGURE 4.46 *Finished shirttail edge*

7. Backstitch at the end
8. Remove from the machine, trim threads
9. Iron
10. Repeat on the other side of the garment

HEMMING THE SIDE VENTS

The last steps finish the garment on the portion below the side seams. These vents have a shirttail finish with some special detailing at the apex of the vent (see Figures 4.47–4.49).

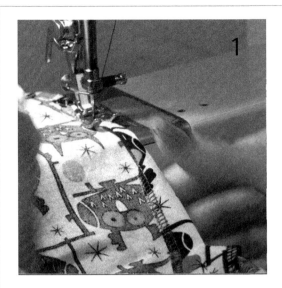

FIGURE 4.47 *Stitch the vents with a shirttail hem*

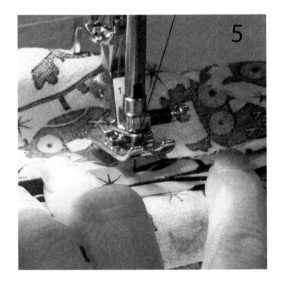

FIGURE 4.48 *Pivot 90° a few stitches above the side seam*

1. On the vent, fold the overlock in two times to the wrong side
   a. The second fold is the ironed edge created after the side seams were sewn
2. Backstitch
3. Stitch up toward the side seam and a couple stitches past the side seam
4. With the needle down, lift the presser foot
5. Pivot the fabric 90°
6. Prep the upcoming seam allowance with two folds
7. Lower the presser foot and sew over the top of the side seam from one edge of the fold to the other edge of the fold
8. On the edge of the next folded area, stop with the needle down

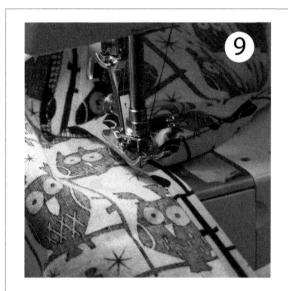

FIGURE 4.49 *Pivot again to stitch down the vent*

9. Lift the presser foot and pivot 90°
10. Stitch to the end of the shirttail hem
11. Backstitch
12. Repeat on the other side of the shirt

Press the shirt one last time before wearing. Include a photograph of the scrub shirt in your portfolio.

Pictured: Hope O'Reilly, Andrew Patterson, Heather Wallman, and Abigail Smith wearing their scrub shirts

REVIEW

- At chest size 44" and fabric 60" wide, how much fabric should you buy for scrub shirt B Top?
- How much ease is in a size small shirt worn by an actor with a chest measurement of 40?
- Describe the process of putting a pattern piece on the grain.
- When a pattern specifies that a piece is placed on the fold, should the folded edge be cut open?
- Is the double notch or the single notch the indicator for the back of the sleeve?

CHAPTER 5
HOUR FOURTEEN

These last two quick hours are both review and reinforcement. Put your skills to use with the construction of a tote bag. The directions are becoming brief. If necessary, go back and review previous exercises. The portfolio shows the progression of skills and the depth of your accomplishments.

NECESSARY SUPPLIES FOR CHAPTER 5*

One standard-sized plastic bag with handles

About one yard of woven fabric

- The measurement from selvage to selvage (width) should be 45″ or more
- Cotton canvas, broadcloth, or denim work very well. Perhaps there is an opportunity to upcycle fabric from a discarded item

One piece of full sized newspaper – or other large piece of paper

Yardstick

Desired medium for portfolio (three-ring binder, large binder, electronic format, website)

*Plus previously introduced supplies

TOTE BAG

Follow the tote bag section and note the new vs. familiar sewing techniques.

FIGURE 5.2 *Use a plastic bag to create a pattern*

FIGURE 5.3 *Lengthen the handles*

This sections creates a pattern (see Figures 5.2 and 5.3). Once created, the paper pattern will last for several projects. Cutting up more plastic will not be necessary.

1. To create the pattern, deconstruct a plastic shopping bag
   a. Along the bottom, and at the top of the handles, cut open a plastic shopping bag, unfurl any folds, and separate the two layers. One layer creates the pattern
2. Trace around the shape of the bag onto a large sheet of paper (I use newspaper)
   a. Use a ruler or yardstick to keep your lines straight
   b. Be a little generous around the edges for seam allowance. The seam allowance and other measurements are not exact because this item doesn't fit on a body like a garment.
3. Lengthen the handles by drawing the cutting line 2"–3" above the top edge of the handle on the plastic bag

FIGURE 5.4 *Place the pattern on the fabric*

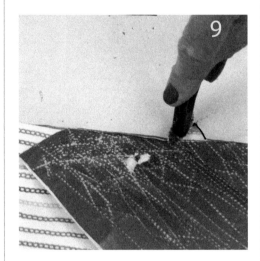

FIGURE 5.5 *Transfer the marks*

4. At the bottom of the bag, draw a notch where the plastic was pleated
    a. There will be two notches on the pattern at the bottom of the bag
5. On the sides of the bag, where the handle ends and the sides begin, draw an X

This section outlines cutting and marking the fabric (see Figures 5.4 and 5.5):

6. Fold the fabric in half and lay it on a large surface
    a. Place the selvages on top of each other
    b. Keep the wrong side of the fabric together
7. Place the pattern on the fabric
    a. Keep either the side of the bag or the bottom edge of the bag parallel to the selvage
8. Cut out the bag shape through both layers of fabric
9. Transfer the notches and two X marks to the wrong side of both layers of the fabric
    a. This technique is the same as the scrub shirt. Fold the

FIGURE 5.6 *Overlock each piece*

FIGURE 5.7 *Sew the top of the handles*

tracing paper in half so that the ink is on the top and bottom. Place the tracing paper between the layers of cut tote bag shapes. Use a tracing wheel to mark the fabric

This section describes the bag assembly (see Figures 5.6–5.16):

10. Separate the two layers of tote bag pieces
11. Overlock
12. With right sides together, stitch the top of the handles
    a. This is similar to straight stitching the shoulder seams of the scrub shirt

FIGURE 5.8 *Stitch the sides from X to the bottom of the bag*

13. With right sides together, stitch the sides of the bag from the X to the bottom
    a. This is similar to the side seams of the scrub shirt
    b. Backstitching is very important in maintaining the integrity of the bag when loaded

FIGURE 5.9 *Iron open the seam allowances*

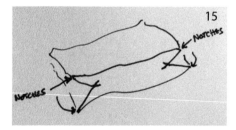

FIGURE 5.10 *Sketch shows the pleat at the bottom of the bag*

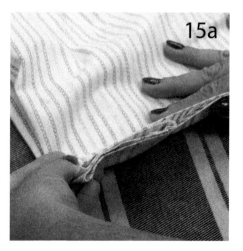

FIGURE 5.11 *Keep the raw edges even at the seam allowance*

14. Press open all four of those seams
    a. Use a sleeve board if available
    b. Leave the bag wrong side out
15. To create the pleat at the bottom of the bag, fold in the side seams. The outside edge is now at the notch
    a. Keep the raw edges of the bottom aligned
    b. Pin to hold the layers together and stacked

16. Sew a straight stitch along the bottom through all layers
17. With slightly less seam allowance, sew a second straight stitch seam along the bottom through all layers
    a. This double stitching strengthens the bag

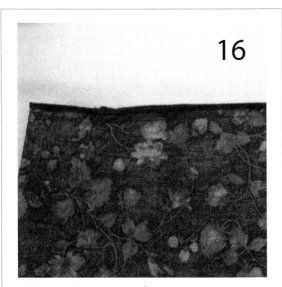

FIGURE 5.12 *Stitch at 5/8". Backstitch*

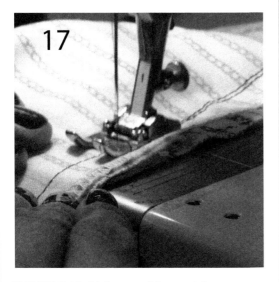

FIGURE 5.13 *Stitch a second time to reinforce*

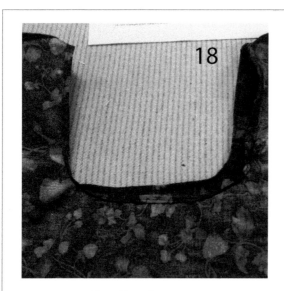

FIGURE 5.14 *Shirttail hem the opening*

FIGURE 5.15 *Pivot at top of side seams*

18. Shirttail hem around the large top opening of the bag
    a. The curves are tricky
    b. Prepare the double fold about 1"–2" ahead of the needle
    c. Overlap the beginning and ending stitches to prevent unraveling
19. Shirttail hem the handle openings at each side
    a. The shirttail hem across the side seam is similar to the hem above the vents on the scrub shirt

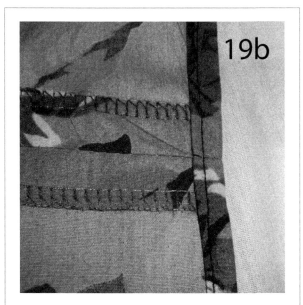

FIGURE 5.16 *Splay seam allowance a the top of the handles*

b. Keep the seam allowances from the top of the handle splayed when shirttail hemming

c. Overlap the beginning and ending stitches to prevent unraveling

20. Iron all of the shirttail hemmed edges

FIGURE 5.17 *Student Kelsey Mattos with her tote bag*

Take a picture of this item for display in your portfolio. Remember to bring your bag along when shopping.

HOUR FIFTEEN

PORTFOLIO

Most artists have a portfolio. In the form of an extra large display case, slide show, or website, they can take on any shape and medium. To keep it basic, these directions cover a three-ring binder that displays the sample stitches and contains a picture of the scrub shirt and tote bag.

Portfolio Requirements

Recognize that the portfolio itself is a work of art and therefore has many personalizations. There is a short list of parameters and within these are millions of interpretations (see Figures 5.18–5.21).

This portfolio project should contain the following:

—A cover page that titles the portfolio and names the creator

FIGURE 5.18 *Cover page*

FIGURE 5.19 *Hand stitching sample*

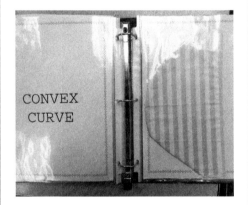

FIGURE 5.20 *Machine stitching sample*

FIGURE 5.21 *Photograph of scrub shirt*

—Clear plastic sheet protectors that hold the stitching samples and the project titles. Everything in the portfolio should be contained in the sheet protectors

—Printed titles to label the various stitches

—Consider using card stock in the page protectors to anchor the sewing samples

—A little piece of clear tape at the opening of the page protector will prevent the contents from spilling out

—Consistent page orientation – avoid flipping from portrait to landscape

—Layout design – the right and left of the binding contain matching subject matter

—High quality photo(s) of completed project(s)

—Professional appeal

CONCLUSION

Congratulations stitcher! Sewing is a difficult skill to master. Now, with your scrub shirt, tote bag, and portfolio in hand, you are ready for more costume shop excitement.

REVIEW

- What part of the tote bag was the most challenging?
- When will you use your tote bag?
- What did you learn from completing the portfolio?
- What do you want to sew next?

MASTER SUPPLY LIST

NECESSARY SUPPLIES FOR CHAPTER 1

Fabric scissors
Thread scissors
Measuring tape
Chalk
1 yard of woven fabric
Overlock sewing machine

NECESSARY SUPPLIES FOR CHAPTER 2

Thread
Hand sewing needle
Flat button – four holes
Shank button
Snap (two parts)
Skirt hook and bar
Seam gauge

Pins
Iron

NECESSARY SUPPLIES FOR CHAPTER 3

Sewing machine
Sewing machine manual
Tailor's ham
Tracing paper
Tracing wheel
Point turner
10" of single fold bias tape

NECESSARY SUPPLIES FOR CHAPTER 4

Simplicity Pattern #4101 (it comes in sizes XS–XL and XL–XXXL)

About 2.5 yards of woven fabric
- The measurement from selvage to selvage (width) should be 45" or more

NECESSARY SUPPLIES FOR CHAPTER 5

One standard-sized plastic bag with handles

About one yard of woven fabric
- The measurement from selvage to selvage (width) should be 45" or more
- Cotton canvas, broadcloth, or denim work very well. Perhaps there is an opportunity to upcycle fabric from a discarded item

One piece of full sized newspaper – or other large piece of paper

Yardstick

Desired medium for portfolio (three-ring binder, large binder, electronic format, website)

CHAPTER REVIEW ANSWERS

CHAPTER 1

Review

True/False

_____Millinery and crafts are never done in a costume shop.

   A. False, millinery and other crafts are often done in the costume shop.

_____Sewing machines are the most important things in a shop.

   A. False, people are the most important things in the costume shop.

_____Partnering with an experienced stitcher can be helpful in the short and long term.

   A. True, collaborating can benefit the experienced and the new stitcher.

_____Safety is the responsibility of the costume shop manager.

   A. False, safety is the responsibility of everyone in the costume shop.

_____Costume shops should celebrate their accomplishments.

   A. True, there is power in community and reflection.

Review

True/False

_____This book divides fabric into four basic types.

   A. True, it is a simplification, yet fabric divides into four basic types.

_____The grain of the fabric has more stretch than the bias.

   A. False, the grain has the least amount of stretch in woven fabric.

_____The bias has less stretch than the cross grain.

   A. False, the bias has the most stretch in woven fabric.

_____The overlock machine has an auto shutoff to prevent cuts.

A. False, be careful with this machine because it can cut your fingers.

_____ The overlock machine only has one cone of thread.

A. False, the overlock machine has at least three cones of thread.

CHAPTER 2

Review

- Describe the orientation of a skirt hook to the finished edge of the garment.

   A. The hook lays flat with the fold of the hook parallel and near the fold of the fabric's edge.

- Name the two parts of a snap.

   A. The snap consists of the socket and the stud.

- What are some of the factors to consider when selecting the correct size snap?

   A. A snap should be strong enough to hold the fabric yet discreet.

- Which hemming stitch is nearly invisible from the right and wrong side of the fabric?

   A. The slip stitch is nearly invisible from the inside and outside of the garment.

- When is it best to use the whip stitch to hem a costume?

   A. Use a whip stitch for quick repairs when only one side of the garment is going to be visible.

CHAPTER 3

Review

- Rethread the sewing machine. Time yourself on this task. Can you do it in under two minutes?

   A. Practice will improve threading time.

- Why are seams backstitched?

   A. Backstitching locks the seam to prevent unraveling.

- Name some uses for top stitching.

   A. Top stitching adds detail, reduces the bulk of a seam allowance, or dictates a garment's fold.

- What is *grading the seam*?

   A. Grading the seam trims one layer of the seam allowance to half of the original width.

- Why are curves clipped or notched?

   A. Clipping and notching manages the seam allowances resisting necessary folds and finishes.

- Is the concave curve notched or clipped?

   A. Concave curves are clipped to allow the seam allowance to splay.

- Describe the three cuts needed on the seam allowance at the tip of a 90° corner.

   A. Trim the tip parallel to the 45° stitch. On both sides of the first cut, trim the seam allowance again, dividing the fabric remaining from the first clip by half.

CHAPTER 4

Review

- At chest size 44" and fabric 60" wide, how much fabric should you buy for scrub shirt B Top?

    A. Purchase 2 yards.

- How much ease is in a size small shirt worn by an actor with a chest measurement of 40?

    A. There is 9" of ease.

- Describe the process of putting a pattern piece on the grain.

    A. To put a pattern piece on grain (a piece that does not need to be cut on the fold), measure from one end of the double arrow to the selvage. Shift the other end of the double arrow until it measures the same distance from the selvage.

- When a pattern specifies that a piece is placed on the fold, should the folded edge be cut open?

    A. No, cutting it open will negate the intended shape of the piece.

- Is the double notch or the single notch the indicator for the back of the sleeve?

    A. A double notch on the cap (rounded edge) of a sleeve indicates the back.

CHAPTER 5

Review

- What part of the tote bag was the most challenging?
- When will you use your tote bag?
- What did you learn from completing the portfolio?
- What do you want to sew next?

    A. All of Chapter 5's answers will vary.

INDEX

Note: **Boldface** page references indicate boxed text. *Italic* references indicate figures.

backstitching 62–66, *63*, *64*, *65*, *66*, *67*
balance wheel 57, *57*
Bernina sewing machine 56, *58*, **58**
bias of fabric 7, *7*
bias tape, hemming with 94–96, *95*, *96*, *97*
bobbin 57, *57*
bobbin casing 57, *57*
bobbin door 57, *57*
buttons: completed sample 32, *32*; flat 28–31, *29*, *30*, *31*; shank 24–27, *25*, *26*, *27*

chalk, marking fabric with **28**
completed samples or projects *see* portfolio
concave curve seams 73–76, *73*, *74*, *75*, *76*, *77*
convex curve seams 77–79, *78*, *79*, *80*
costume construction 4; *see also* fabric; *specific technique*
costume shop: elements 1–2; party at 4; safety 3–4, *3*
cross grain (woof) of fabric 7–8, *7*
curved seams: completed samples 77, *80*; concave 73–76, *73*, *74*, *75*, *76*, *77*; convex 77–79, *78*, *79*, *80*; simple 71–72, *72*

darts 85–93, *86*, *87*, *88*, *89*, *90*, *91*, *92*, *93*, *94*, **94**

fabric: bias of 7, *7*; buying 8, *8*, **8**, **102**; categories of 5–7, *6*; cross grain of 7–8, *7*; dividing 8–10, *9*; felt 5–6, *6*; grain of 7, *7*; knit 5–6, *6*; leather 5–6, *6*; marking (with chalk or wax) **28**; measuring 8, *8*; overlocking edges of 20, *20*, 109–110, *110*; pivoting **113**; selvage of 7, *7*, 10, *10*, **11**; sides of, right and wrong 44, *45*, **45–46**; supplies **5**; wider, cost of **102**; woven 5–7, *6*
facings, stitching shoulder seams on 112, *112*
fasteners: completed sample 44, *44*; hook-and-bar 32–37, *33*, *34*, *35*, *36*, *37*; snaps 38–43, *38*, *39*, *40*, *42*, *43*
felt fabric 5–6, *6*
fire extinguisher 3, *3*
flat buttons 28–31, *29*, *30*, *31*
foot pedal 57, *57*

grain (warp) of fabric 7, *7*

hand sewing needles 21
hand sewing samples: buttons 24–32, *25*, *26*, *27*, *29*, *30*, *31*, *32*; fasteners 32–44, *33*, *34*, *35*, *36*, *37*, *38*, *39*, *40*, *42*, *43*, *44*; hemming stitches 46–52, *47*, *48*, *49*, *50*, *51*, *52*, *53*
hemming: with bias tape 94–96, *95*, *96*, *97*; side vents 130–132, *131*, *132*; sleeves 128–132, *128*, *129*, *130*, *131*, *132*
hemming stitches: completed sample 53; overview 46; shirttail 129, *129*, *130*, 142–143, *142*, *143*; slip stitch 50–52, *50*, *51*, *52*; whip stitch 46–49, *47*, *48*, *49*, *50*
hook-and-bar fasteners: bar 32–35, *33*, *34*, *35*; function of 32; hook 36–37, *36*, *37*

irons 32

knives on overlock sewing machine 12, 13, *13*
knit fabric 5–6, *6*
knotting thread 21, 23, *23*

Index

leather fabric 5–6, *6*

machine sewing needles 21
machine sewing samples *see* sewing machine samples
marking fabric (with chalk or wax) **28**
measuring fabric 8, *8*

neckline, finishing edge 113–120, *113, 114, 115, 116, 117, 118, 119, 120*
needles: hand 21; knotting threaded 21, 23, *23*; sewing machine 21; threading 21, *22*, **24**
91° corner 80–84, *81, 82, 83, 84, 85*
non-overlock sewing machine *see* sewing machine
notions, sewing 21; *see also specific type*

overlocking: alternatives to **16**; edges of fabric 20, *20*, 109–110, *110*; scrub shirt project 109–110, *110*; supplies **19**; tote bag project 138, *138*
overlock sewing machine: knives *12, 13*, **13**; names for 11; overview 11–13; parts 13, *13*; practicing sewing on 13–15, *14, 15*; presser foot 13, *13*; presser foot lifter 13, *13*

pattern, reading 100–102, *100, 103*
pinking shears or scissors **16**
pinning and attaching sleeves 121–123, *121, 122, 123*
pivoting fabric **113**
portfolio: button samples 32, *32*; curved seam samples 77, *80*; dart sample *94*; fastener samples 44, **44**; hand stitching samples *145*; hemming with bias tape sample *97*; hemming stitches sample *53*; machine stitching samples *145*; 91° corner sample *85*; overview 16, **17**; photograph of scrub shirt in *145*; requirements 144–145; scrub shirt project *132, 145*;

straight stitch seams sample 67, 71; title or cover page 17, *144*; tote bag project *143*
presser foot 13, *13*, 57, *57*
presser foot lifter or lever 13, *13*, 57, *57*
Pro Tips: alternatives to overlocking **16**; buying fabric 8, **102**; darts **94**; function of, xii; measuring fabric 8; pivoting fabric **113**; seam allowance **80**; selvage, removing **11**; sides of fabric, right and wrong **45–46**; threading sewing machine **58**

regular sewing machine *see* sewing machine
reverse lever on sewing machine 57, *57*

safety: costume shop 3–4, *3*; irons and 32
scrub shirt project: completed *132*; cutting out 102, 107–109, *107, 108, 109*; laying out 102, 104–106, *104, 105, 106*; neckline, finishing edge 113–120, *113, 114, 115, 116, 117, 118, 119, 120*; overlocking edges 109–110, *110*; pattern 100–102, *100, 103*; shoulder seams, stitching 110–112, *111, 112*; side seams, stitching 124–127, *124, 125, 126, 127*; sleeves, hemming 128–132, *128, 129, 130, 131, 132*; sleeves, pinning and attaching 121–123, *121, 122, 123*; supplies **99**
seam allowance **80**
seam allowance guidelines on throat plate 57, *57*
selvage of fabric 7, *7, 10*, *10*, **11**
sewing machine: as alternative to overlocking **16**; Bernina 56, 58, **58**; historical perspective 56; modern 56; needles 21; parts 57, *57*; supplies **55**; threading 58, *58*, **58**

sewing machine samples: backstitching 62–63, *63, 64*; curved seams 71–85, *72, 73, 74, 75, 76, 77, 78, 79*; darts 85–93, *86, 87, 88, 89, 90, 91, 92, 93, 94*, **94**; hemming with bias tape 94–96, *95, 96, 97*; 91° corner 80–84, *81, 82, 83, 84, 85*; straight stitch seam 59–70, *60, 61, 63, 64, 65, 66, 67, 68, 69, 70*; top stitching 67–70, *68, 69, 70*; *see also* scrub shirt project; tote bag project
sewing notions 21; *see also specific type*
shank buttons 24–27, *25, 26, 27*
shirt *see* scrub shirt project
shirttail hem: scrub shirt project 129, *129, 130*; tote bag project 142–143, *142, 143*
shoulder seams 110–112, *111, 112*
side seams 124–127, *124, 125, 126, 127*
sides of fabric, right and wrong 44, *45*, **45–46**
side vents, hemming 130–132, *131, 132*
sleeves: hemming 128–132, *128, 129, 130, 131, 132*; pinning and attaching 121–123, *121, 122, 123*
slip stitch 50–52, *50, 51, 52*
snaps: function of 38; socket 38, 39–40, *39, 40*; stud 38, 41–43, *42, 43*
spray booth 3, *3*
straight stitch seam: backstitching and 62–66, *63, 64, 65, 66, 67*; completed samples *67, 71*; technique 59–61, *60, 61*; top stitching and 67–70, *68, 69, 70, 71*
straight stitch sewing machine *see* sewing machine
supplies: fabric **5**; master list 147–148; overlocking **19**; scrub shirt **99**; sewing machine **55**; tote bag project **135**; *see also specific type*

threading needles: hand 21, 22, **24**; knotting 21, 23, *23*; machine 58, *58*, **58**
threads 21
top stitching 67–70, *68*, *69*, *70*, *71*
tote bag project: bottom pleat 140, *140*; bottom reinforcement 141, *141*; completed *143*; cutting pattern 137–138, *138*; handles 138, *138*; overlocking 138, *138*; pattern, creating 136, *136*; shirttail hem top and handles 142–143, *142*, *143*; sides 139, *139*; supplies **135**; tracing pattern 136–137, *137*

vent hood over dye vat 3, *3*

warp (grain) of fabric 7, *7*
wax, marking fabric with **28**
whip stitch 46–49, *47*, *48*, *49*, *50*
woof (cross-grain) of fabric 7–8, *7*
woven fabric 5–7, *6*

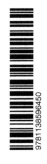